VINCENZO VENEZIA

insecure attachment

Anxious or Avoidant in Love? Understand Your Attachment Style and Create Secure Emotional Connections

© Copyright 2023 Vincenzo Venezia - **All rights reserved.**

The content contained within this book may not be reproduced, duplicated or transmitted without direct written permission from the author or the publisher.

Under no circumstances will any blame or legal responsibility be held against the publisher, or author, for any damages, reparation, or monetary loss due to the information contained within this book; either directly or indirectly.

Legal Notice:

This book is copyright protected. This book is only for personal use. You cannot amend, distribute, sell, use, quote or paraphrase any part, or the content within this book, without the consent of the author or publisher.

Disclaimer Notice:

Please note the information contained within this document is for educational and entertainment purposes only. All effort has been executed to present accurate, up-to-date, and reliable, complete information. No warranties of any kind are declared or implied. Readers acknowledge that the author is not engaging in the rendering of legal, financial, medical or professional advice.

ISBN: 979-12-81498-51-8

Contents

Introduction	1
Chapter 1: Early Theories of Attachment	5
Chapter 2: Childhood Trauma and Insecure Attachment: The Connection Between Pain and Relationships	13
Chapter 3: The Pillars of Love: Creating a Deep and Meaningful Connection	22
Chapter 4: Anxious Attachment	38
Chapter 5: Avoidant Attachment	50
Chapter 6: Disorganized Attachment	62
Chapter 7: Insecure Attachment Subtypes: Understanding the Different Ways We Bond	73
Chapter 8: What's Your Attachment Style?	92
Chapter 9: Overcoming Barriers to Change	103
Chapter 10: Building Trust and Intimacy in Romantic Relationships	114
Chapter 11: Cultivating a Secure Base in Relationships	132

Chapter 12: Becoming Your Own Secure Base: Fostering 156
Self-Love and Unleashing Your Authenticity

Chapter 13: Addressing Past Trauma and Attachment Wounds 167

Conclusion 186

Introduction

Did you know that over 50% of adults experience repeating patterns of emotional turbulence in their romantic relationships? Despite their best intentions, they find themselves trapped in a perpetual cycle of insecurity, misunderstanding, and heartache. But what lies at the core of this distressing pattern?

The roots of *"Insecure Attachment"* reach deep into the annals of psychology, discovered in the mid-20th century in the work of British psychologist John Bowlby. This seminal work reveals the hallmarks of romantic relationships and explores the intricate patterns of anxious, avoidant, and disorganized attachments that plague those who seek love. From incessant neediness to the fear of rejection, the struggles faced by those with insecure attachments can seem insurmountable.

Romantic relationships can be a source of great joy and fulfillment, but they can also be challenging if attachment issues are unresolved. Insecure attachment can lead to a variety of problems, including communication breakdowns, fear of intimacy, emotional distance, jealousy, and an incessant sense of insecurity. These issues can lead to cycles of conflict and emotional turmoil, undermining the foundation of trust and security that is essential for a thriving relationship.

Insecure attachment can manifest itself in many ways, making it difficult to trust your partner and leaving you constantly questioning their intentions. This lack of trust can hinder the building of intimacy and closeness, leading to frustration and resentment in your relationship. In addition, you may find it difficult to communicate your needs and feelings to your partner, fearing rejection or abandonment if you express your true emotions.

For some, insecure attachment can lead to self-destructive behaviors as a way of coping with the anxiety and pain it causes. While these behaviors may provide temporary relief, they can exacerbate problems in the long run. In addition, failure to address insecure attachment can lead to difficulties forming and maintaining healthy relationships, low self-esteem, and mental health problems such as depression and anxiety.

If you are reading this book, you are probably wondering about insecure attachment. What is it? How does it affect our relationships? These are just some of the questions that people with insecure attachment ask themselves.

Or you might want to ask yourself:

Why do I always feel so anxious or avoidant in my relationships?

Am I deserving of love and affection?

How can I trust others when I have been hurt in the past?

I'm guessing you have some other questions that you're thinking about, such as:

Why am I constantly seeking reassurance and confirmation from others?

What can I do to stop feeling so dependent on others for my happiness?

Why do I attract partners who seem emotionally unavailable or distant?

How can I form healthy and secure bonds with others?

What is it about me that makes it difficult to maintain stable relationships?

Why do I struggle to express my emotions and needs to others?

How can I build my self-confidence and self-esteem?

What steps can I take to heal from past attachment wounds?

If you are asking yourself any of these questions, then this book is for you. It will help you understand insecure attachment and how it affects your life.

This work offers guidance and understanding for those who find themselves caught up in the repetitive patterns of insecure attachment. Whether you're single, dating, or committed, the insights shared here will empower you to recognize, confront, and transform the insecure attachment patterns that hinder your ability to form secure and fulfilling bonds.

This resource is not intended to replace the counsel of a qualified mental health professional. If you are dealing with severe emotional challenges, seeking the support of a licensed mental health professional is essential. However, this resource can provide a starting point for understanding different attachment styles and how they affect your relationships. It can also help you develop the self-awareness and skills you need to build more secure and enriching relationships.

This book is unique in its multifaceted approach to insecure attachment. Rather than focusing solely on clinical symptoms and treatment, it brings to light the human experiences that lie beneath the surface. Recognizing the whole person with their needs, desires, and experiences, Insecure Attachment offers a compassionate understanding of the complexities of attachment theory. In doing so, it provides valuable insights for fostering self-awareness, emotional growth, and the development of secure and enriching relationships.

However, this book is not intended to be a magic bullet. There is no quick fix for insecure attachment, and it takes time, effort, and commitment to make lasting changes. This book can provide you with a starting point, but it is up to you to do the work.

The exercises and activities in this book are designed to help you explore your attachment style, understand your triggers, and develop new coping mechanisms. They are not meant to be easy, but they are essential if you want to make lasting change.

Remember, you are not alone. Millions of people struggle with insecure attachment, and there is hope for healing. With the tools and support in this book, you can overcome your challenges and build the relationships you truly deserve.

Chapter 1: Early Theories of Attachment

What lies at the heart of our deepest emotional connections? When we talk about attachment, we open the door to a realm that touches the very core of human existence-the bonds that bind us together, the emotions that shape us, and the attachments that leave an indelible mark on our lives. It all begins with a profound question: why do we, as social beings, form such enduring and powerful emotional bonds with others? In this chapter, we embark on a journey of discovery to uncover the origins of attachment theory, tracing its roots back to the fascinating world of evolutionary psychology.

Many millennia ago, our ancestors roamed the earth in tight-knit groups where survival was intimately tied to the strength of their social bonds. It was against this backdrop of communal interdependence that the seeds of attachment were sown. The human brain, a remarkable product of evolution, developed a remarkable capacity-the instinctive desire to seek closeness, comfort, and security from our caregivers or loved ones.

Imagine our distant ancestors huddled around a fire, sharing warmth and protection. From the earliest days of humanity, we have craved the reassurance of companionship-a source of comfort in times of need, a beacon of hope in the face of uncertainty. These emotional bonds were far more than mere sentiments; they were a matter of survival and the very foundation of our species' continuity.

Yet it was not until the mid-20th century that a brilliant mind named John Bowlby began to unravel the intricacies of human attachment in a systematic and groundbreaking way. Drawing from various fields, including biology, ethology, and psychoanalysis, Bowlby meticulously pieced together the puzzle of attachment theory.

Bowlby's findings challenged traditional views of child development and parenting and offered a new perspective on the importance of emotional bonds in shaping the course of human life. His theory posited that attachment was not merely a byproduct of convenience or necessity, but an integral part of our psychological makeup, influencing our emotional regulation, self-concept, and future relationships.

John Bowlby, a visionary British psychiatrist and psychologist, is considered the architect of attachment theory. Born in London in 1907, Bowlby's early life experiences profoundly influenced his interest in child development and the bonds between caregivers and children. His findings revolutionized our understanding of human relationships and emotional development.

Based on his work with emotionally disturbed children and the effects of World War II on young evacuees, Bowlby recognized the critical role of secure attachments in promoting healthy emotional growth. He believed that children instinctively seek proximity to their primary caregivers, usually their mothers, for comfort, safety, and protection. These attachments, he argued, served as a secure base from which children could explore the world, develop resilience, and form positive relationships throughout their lives.

Bowlby's ideas challenged the prevailing psychoanalytic theories of his time, which often emphasized internal conflicts and intrapsychic processes. Instead, he proposed that the bonds formed between children and their caregivers were a fundamental aspect of human nature, biologically wired to ensure survival and optimal development.

In the 1950s, Bowlby began publishing his seminal works, including "Child Care and the Growth of Love" (1953) and "Separation: Anxiety and Anger" (1973). However, it was his trilogy of books - "Attachment" (1969), "Separation" (1973), and "Loss" (1980) - that solidified attachment theory as a profound and comprehensive framework.

His ideas laid the groundwork for understanding attachment patterns and the lasting impact of early relationships on an individual's emotional and social life. Moreover, Bowlby's theory extended beyond childhood to include attachment patterns in romantic relationships and adulthood, emphasizing that the need for emotional closeness persists throughout life.

Today, Bowlby's seminal work continues to influence fields such as developmental psychology, psychiatry, and counseling. Attachment theory serves as a guiding framework for understanding the formation of human relationships, the impact of early experiences on emotional well-being, and the design of interventions to support individuals with insecure attachment patterns.

Attachment in Infancy: Nurturing the Roots of Trust and Security

Picture this: a baby in a room with a caregiver and a stranger. The caregiver leaves, and the baby's reaction to this separation becomes a window into the world of attachment. How do infants bond with their parents? What factors shape their feelings of security and trust? These questions have fascinated psychologists and researchers for decades.

In the mid-20th century, the pioneering work of John Bowlby laid the foundation for our understanding of attachment theory. Bowlby's research and findings highlighted the importance of early emotional bonds between infants and their primary caregivers. He emphasized that these bonds were vital to a child's healthy emotional development and set the stage for their future relationships.

Enter Mary Ainsworth, a key figure who would further expand and enrich Bowlby's attachment theory. Influenced by Bowlby's ideas, Ainsworth became a close collaborator and colleague. She was a brilliant developmental psychologist who sought to empirically test and refine attachment theory.

The "Strange Situation" experiment, conducted in the 1970s, involved observing how infants between the ages of 12 and 18 months responded to separation and reunion with their primary caregivers in a controlled yet sensitive environment. This experiment allowed researchers to identify distinct attachment patterns based on the child's behavior during the process.

Through her astute observations and analysis, Mary Ainsworth uncovered three primary attachment styles:

- Secure attachment: Babies who exhibit secure attachment feel safe exploring their environment when their caregiver is present. When the caregiver leaves, they may experience distress, but they are easily comforted when the caregiver returns. This secure base allows them to venture out into the world, knowing that they can seek comfort and support when needed.

- Insecure-Avoidant Attachment: In this attachment style, babies appear independent and self-sufficient, seemingly indifferent to the presence or absence of their caregiver. They may not seek comfort from the caregiver when they are distressed and may display a more aloof demeanor.

- Insecure-Ambivalent/Resistant Attachment: Babies with this attachment style often exhibit clingy and hesitant behavior and become very distressed when the caregiver leaves. When the caregiver returns, they may remain anxious and difficult to soothe, showing a mixture of seeking comfort and expressing anger or resistance.

Originally, Mary Ainsworth used the term "resistant attachment" to describe this attachment style in her "Strange Situation" experiment, while other researchers and later studies began using the term "anxious attachment" to refer to the same style. Over time, "anxious attachment" became a more commonly used term in the research and clinical literature.

Mary Ainsworth's work significantly complemented and extended John Bowlby's original ideas, providing empirical evidence for the existence of different attachment styles and their impact on child development. Her research highlighted the critical role of caregivers in the formation of secure attachments and deepened our understanding of the complexity of the infant-parent relationship.

The discovery of new subtypes

After Mary Ainsworth's groundbreaking work, attachment theory continued to evolve through the contributions of other key figures, leading to the identification of additional subtypes of attachment and a more comprehensive understanding of its impact on human relationships.

One such notable figure is Mary Main, an American psychologist and collaborator with Ainsworth. Main's work took attachment theory to new heights by identifying a new subtype of attachment known as "disorganized" attachment. Disorganized attachment refers to a pattern in which children exhibit inconsistent or disoriented behavior in response to the absence and return of their caregiver. These children may exhibit a mixture of seeking comfort from the caregiver while also displaying avoidant or anxious behaviors. Main's research highlighted the importance of considering not only the nature of the attachment styles identified by Ainsworth (secure, insecure-avoidant, or insecure-ambivalent/resistant), but also the presence of disorganized behaviors in some children. This nuanced approach added depth to attachment theory by recognizing that some children may experience more complex and confusing responses in their attachment relationships.

Attachment theory has expanded to include additional subtypes, such as fearful avoidant attachment and dismissive avoidant attachment styles. These subtypes provide valuable insights into the complexity of attachment patterns and their impact on an individual's emotional experiences and relationships.

The fearful-avoidant attachment style was first studied in the 1980s by researchers such as Mary Ainsworth's colleague, Solomon and George. Fearful avoidant individuals exhibit a combination of anxiety and avoidance in close relationships. They desire emotional closeness and intimacy but are also afraid of being hurt or rejected, so they avoid or withdraw from relationships to protect themselves from potential emotional pain.

Dismissive avoidant attachment was also studied by researchers in the 1980s and is associated with a strong emphasis on independence and self-reliance. Individuals with this attachment style tend to downplay the importance of close relationships and may appear emotionally distant or detached from others. They often avoid seeking support or comfort from others in times of distress and may prefer to manage their emotions on their own.

In addition, researchers and scholars such as Heidi Keller and Kim Bartholomew further enriched attachment theory by exploring cultural variations in attachment patterns. While attachment theory emerged from studies conducted in Western societies, these researchers examined how attachment manifests in different cultural contexts. They discovered culturally specific attachment patterns that emphasized the influence of cultural norms, values, and parenting practices on attachment styles. This expanded view of attachment highlighted the importance of considering cultural diversity when studying attachment relationships and their impact on child development.

In furthermore, attachment theory expanded beyond infancy and childhood to include adult attachment styles. Psychologists such as Cindy Hazan and Phillip Shaver applied attachment theory to the study of romantic relationships. Through their research, they identified three main adult attachment styles: secure, anxious, and avoidant, which mirrored the attachment patterns observed in infancy. This work shed light on how early attachment experiences continue to shape adult romantic relationships, providing valuable insights for understanding relationship dynamics and challenges.

As attachment theory continued to evolve, researchers and practitioners used its principles to develop attachment-based interventions and therapeutic approaches. These interventions aimed to support individuals with insecure attachment patterns and promote more secure and satisfying relationships. By recognizing the impact of early experiences on later life, attachment-based interventions provided a framework for healing and growth.

In summary, the expansion of attachment theory since the foundational work of John Bowlby and Mary Ainsworth has been remarkable. The identification of disorganized attachment, the exploration of cultural variations, the study of adult attachment styles, and the application of attachment-based interventions have collectively contributed to a deeper and more comprehensive understanding of how attachment shapes human relationships from infancy through adulthood. This multifaceted perspective continues to illuminate the intricate dynamics of emotional connections, enriching our knowledge of human behavior and the power of attachment in shaping our lives.

I hope you have found this timeline of the development of psychoanalytic theory informative. In the next chapter we will discuss the invisible wounds of childhood that can have a lasting impact on our adult relationships. This theory suggests that even seemingly small or insignificant childhood experiences can have a profound effect on our emotional development and our ability to form healthy adult relationships.

In the next chapter, we will explore the factors that contribute to insecure attachment. We will look at how childhood experiences can leave lasting marks on our emotional landscape, influencing how we navigate intimacy, trust, and vulnerability in our adult lives.

Chapter 2: Childhood Trauma and Insecure Attachment: The Connection Between Pain and Relationships

How we develop as adults can be greatly influenced by our experiences as children. If we have a bad childhood, we may grow up to be unhappy. Most people who have relationship problems are insecure because they were abused as children. Children are very vulnerable, and the emotional or physical pain they experience stays with them for a long time. Here are some things that children can go through that can be traumatic.

Abandonment

Children are vulnerable. They need to grow up in the warmth of parents who care about them. However, some children are unlucky in the sense that they have parents who don't care about them. Their parents may have a tendency to leave them for long periods of time or be emotionally distant. Things never go well. For emotional stability, children need to spend time with both parents. Children who struggle with abandonment issues find it increasingly difficult to fit into society, and this can lead to a variety of mental health problems.

The loss of a loved one

We are only mortals. We have to leave this planet at some point. But the problem is that some people leave the planet even though they are responsible for other people. Because they lack the necessary emotional stability, children who lose a loved one, especially a parent, may have a difficult time adjusting to society. Losing a loved one can also cause a child to have a bad attitude because they think the world is out to get them. This can lead them down the wrong path.

Natural disasters

As long as we keep doing stupid things that hurt Mother Earth, nature will find ways to strike back, and you can be sure that when Mother Earth strikes back, there will be a lot of damage. Hurricanes are one of the most common ways Mother Earth strikes back. They hit coastal cities and knock down buildings. Children who see this are traumatized for the rest of their lives. Such a traumatic experience can lead to a variety of emotional problems, including attachment

Refugee experience

Again, the world is relatively stable politically, but there are still people fighting in some parts of the world. Children who are born in these places and have to leave as refugees have a hard time becoming emotionally stable. Refugee camps can't give children the warmth they should have.

Accidents

Accidents are another experience that can send a child into trauma. The more advanced our technology is, the more machines we have to operate and the more danger we put ourselves in. Because they don't know how to process the events, if a child has an accident, like on the road, it could affect them for the rest of their lives. It could make them feel bad about life because they are afraid of the next bad thing that could happen.

Life-threatening diseases

We are so fortunate to have reached a point where most medical problems have been eradicated from the planet. But there are still many diseases. A child who is sick is in a world of pain, and it can traumatize them for the rest of their lives. Children know a lot about what's going on. When they are sick, they can't be a normal child. It makes them less happy. It makes them have a bad attitude

Verbal abuse

Verbal abuse is another experience that can traumatize a child. Most of the time, this happens because one or both of their parents have mental health problems. In most cases, the verbally abusive parent is acting from a place of hurt. But two wrongs don't make a right. It doesn't matter that they were hurt too; they should have enough sense to stop hurting their children and start treating them with more respect. Verbal abuse makes a child deeply resentful. It hurts their self-esteem and makes it difficult for them to fit into society. It also creates insecure attachment issues in them.

Domestic violence

In some dysfunctional homes, parents can be mean. Usually, they start by going after each other, but soon they turn their attention to their children. Children who have been physically abused go through a lot of trauma, and when they are young adults, they have a lot of problems, like not being able to trust people.

When a child experiences pain at the hands of a parent or guardian, it can leave them permanently scarred.

Sexual abuse

This is probably one of the worst things a child can go through. Children who are sexually abused have a hard time fitting in with the rest of society. This is because sexual violence makes a person's emotions unstable. Sexual abuse is one of the most traumatic things that can happen to a person. It also lasts a lifetime. Even if the person gets help, they will still feel like what happened to them is haunting them. A child's life is ruined when they are sexually abused.

Parental mental health issues

Parental mental health problems can have a significant impact on a child's attachment style and emotional development. When parents experience mental health challenges, they may struggle to provide consistent emotional support, attunement, and responsiveness to their child's needs. This can lead to various attachment problems in children that affect their behavior, emotions, and relationships in both childhood and adulthood.

Bullying

Kids can be sweet, but they can also be mean, especially to other kids. Bullying can start when children are young and continue through high school. But it leaves the person who is hurt very sad. Children who have been bullied may have a hard time fitting in and building the emotional stability they need to become independent. They may develop attachment issues that make it hard for them to have normal relationships.

Fear

Fear is a child's first reaction to a traumatic experience. If they feel threatened, they will show signs of fear. For example, if a child is being bullied at school, they may not always tell anyone because they are ashamed of what they are going through, but they will always appear to be afraid for their life. You can see the fear in their eyes and the way they hesitate. They will be very careful about what they say or do.

Anxiety

Anxiety tends to start at a very young age. A traumatic experience that a child goes through is usually the cause of their anxiety. For example, if a child has just lost a parent, they may look around and see that their mom or dad isn't there anymore, which makes them feel anxious. Nothing feels the same. They try to find ways to talk about their pain, but they can't even think about it. Their worry prevents them from getting along with others. They can't be happy because of it. They don't look or act like other children. The pain is real.

Depression

Children can also be sad. It usually happens when a child is going through something scary. They don't have the emotional strength to deal with their feelings and figure out what's going on in their lives, so they shut down. Most depressed children try to hide. They don't want to spend time with their friends or family, and they always stay alone, which isn't easy. In the silence of their room, depressed children may cry. They will also have antisocial tendencies.

Nightmares

Dreams are a way for our minds to figure out what is going on in our lives. When a child is going through something scary, they will often have nightmares. Because they are still trying to figure out what is going on, these nightmares will keep them awake. If a child is having trouble with nightmares, it could be a sign that they are going through something scary. It's also not a good sign if a child has trouble falling asleep; it means they've been through a traumatic event.

Loss of appetite

Since children are constantly growing, they need a lot of energy, which is evident by the fact that they have huge appetites. So if a child is not eating enough, it's a bad sign. It shows the traumatic experience the child is going through. For example, if a child is bullied at school and keeps quiet about it, you might notice that they first withdraw and then lose their appetite. Children should have a big appetite because their bodies need a lot of food. So if a child doesn't seem interested in food, it could be a sign of trauma.

Difficulty making new friends

The inability to form relationships with other people is another clear sign that a child is experiencing trauma. Most of the time, this is because of their worries and fears. Relationships are a big part of our lives and not being able to make good ones is also a bad sign. The child doesn't want to have relationships with other people because they have a wrong view of life. They don't trust people and think that people only cause trouble, so they try to avoid them.

Inability to Trust

When a child experiences trauma at the hands of a person, especially a parent, they will think that people in general want to hurt them and will make it a point to avoid everyone they meet or at least never trust them again. And that's one reason why it's hard for them to connect with other people in a meaningful way. A child with trust issues is a loner because they can only rely on themselves when they are in control of the whole process.

Difficulty concentrating

A child's inability to concentrate is another sign that they are going through a traumatic experience. They have a distant look in their eyes because they are lost in their thoughts about the trauma they are going through and it is hard for them to get over the pain they are feeling.

Poor academic performance

A child going through trauma will have a hard time concentrating on their schoolwork and will get poor grades. They also won't be able to understand what they're learning because most of their mental energy is going to processing the traumatic experiences they're going through.

Risky behavior

In most cases, trauma makes children feel too much and makes them quiet. However, in some cases, children respond to trauma by going overboard. These children will start doing dangerous things to forget their traumatic experiences. Of course, these kinds of actions only set them up for a life of crime, which usually ends badly.

Pain and traumatic experiences

- Traumatic experiences can lead to physical pain in children as a way of expressing emotional distress.

- Unexpressed emotions and somatic memories contribute to psychosomatic pain responses.

Attachment issues and trauma

- Traumatic events can disrupt the formation of secure attachments, resulting in insecure attachment styles.

- Insecurely attached children may fear rejection and have difficulty processing emotions related to trauma.

Effects of unresolved pain and attachment issues

- Unresolved pain and attachment issues can worsen over time if left untreated.

- These issues can interfere with a child's enjoyment of childhood and have lasting effects into adulthood.

- Early intervention, therapeutic support, and a nurturing environment are essential to promoting healing and resilience in children with pain and attachment issues.

Childhood experiences can shape our attachment styles in adulthood.

Traumatic events like abandonment, loss, and abuse can leave lasting scars that affect how we perceive and form relationships with others. It is important to recognize the impact of childhood experiences on our emotional well-being and seek support to heal and grow.

The next chapter will discuss secure attachment, the foundation of healthy relationships.

Understanding the pillars of love and secure attachment will help us build healthier connections with ourselves and others.

Chapter 3: The Pillars of Love: Creating a Deep and Meaningful Connection

Love is like the warm sun shining on our hearts, making us feel alive and connected to each other. It's a fundamental emotion that every human being experiences. You have probably felt it, haven't you?

Love is not just a feeling; it's a mix of emotions, thoughts, and actions. It's like a puzzle with many pieces, each contributing to the whole. That's what makes it so fascinating and complex.

Now here's the exciting part: understanding the main pillars of love. These pillars are like the sturdy foundation that holds a building together. In the world of relationships, they are essential for creating healthy and fulfilling connections with those we care about.

Imagine love as a four pillar structure

- **Emotional Intimacy:** This pillar is about sharing your deepest feelings and thoughts with someone special. It's like opening the door to your heart and letting someone see the real you. When you have emotional intimacy, you feel understood and supported, which strengthens your bond.

- **Trust and Respect:** Imagine trust as the invisible thread that binds two hearts together. It's about believing in each other's honesty and reliability. Respect, on the other hand, is like a gentle breeze that keeps the atmosphere of your relationship peaceful and loving. When trust and respect are present, love can truly flourish.

- **Communication:** Picture communication as the key that unlocks the door to meaningful relationships. It's not just about talking; it's also about active listening and understanding. When you communicate openly and honestly with your loved ones, you build bridges of understanding and empathy.

- **Shared values and goals:** This pillar is like a shared adventure that you embark on together. Having similar values and dreams creates a sense of togetherness and alignment. When you support each other's aspirations and grow together, love becomes a powerful force in your lives.

These pillars are not just random ideas. They are the very essence of love. Let's take a closer look at each one.

Emotional Intimacy

Picture this as opening the doors of your heart and inviting someone special in for a warm cup of tea. It's about sharing your deepest feelings and thoughts that are dear to you. When you have emotional intimacy with someone, it's like having a best friend who really "gets" you, understands you inside and out, and still loves you for who you are.

Imagine the feeling of being truly seen and heard, of baring your soul without fear of judgment. That's the magic of emotional intimacy! When you connect with someone on this level, it's like finding a safe haven - a place where you can be your true self, vulnerability and all.

And guess what? This emotional closeness makes your connection even stronger! When you feel understood and supported, you can face life's challenges together, hand in hand, with unwavering trust in each other. It's like having an unbreakable bond that can withstand life's storms.

Emotional intimacy empowers you to be your true self without the need for masks or pretense. When you feel understood and supported, you experience a deep sense of belonging and validation. It's a feeling of being truly seen and heard, of your soul dancing in harmony with another.

In this space of emotional closeness, you create a haven where trust thrives. It's a sanctuary where you can let your guard down, knowing that your feelings and thoughts will be met with empathy and understanding. This vulnerability fosters an unbreakable bond that grows stronger with each shared moment.

So don't be afraid to open up and share your feelings with those who matter most to you. Nurture emotional intimacy like a delicate flower and watch it blossom into a beautiful garden of love and understanding. Remember, the more you embrace this pillar of love, the more your relationships will blossom with warmth and authenticity.

Let's dive into an example with dialogues to showcase emotional intimacy in action:

Emma and Jack have been together for a couple of years. One evening, they are sitting on the couch, having a heart-to-heart conversation.

Emma: (Looking a bit troubled) "You know, Jack, lately, I've been feeling a bit overwhelmed with everything going on at work. It's been really challenging, and I find myself bringing that stress home with me."

Jack: (Nods empathetically) "I understand, Emma. It can be tough to leave work at work sometimes. I'm here for you, though, and I want you to know that you can talk to me about anything."

Emma: (Taking a deep breath) "Thank you, Jack. I guess I just worry that I'm not handling things well, and I don't want it to affect us."

Jack: "I appreciate you sharing that with me. You're doing great, Emma. We all have tough days, and it's okay to feel overwhelmed. You're not alone in this, and I'm here to support you in any way I can."

Emma: (Softly) "It's just hard to admit that I'm struggling sometimes. I don't want you to see me as weak or incapable."

Jack: (Cupping her hand in his) "Emma, you're not weak. Opening up like this shows strength and trust. I admire your courage to share your feelings with me. It makes me feel closer to you, knowing that we can be vulnerable with each other."

Emma: (Tears welling up) "I'm glad you feel that way, Jack. I love you so much, and I never want anything to come between us."

Jack: "And I love you too, Emma. We're a team, and we'll face whatever comes our way together. Your feelings matter to me, and I promise to be here, no matter what."

In this dialogue, Emma and Jack exemplify emotional intimacy by openly discussing their feelings and concerns. Emma bravely shares her struggles, allowing herself to be vulnerable with Jack. In response, Jack listens attentively, offering reassurance and support, creating a safe space for Emma to express herself.

Trust and Respect

Trust and respect are like the glue that holds two hearts together. They are the very essence of a loving relationship, creating a sense of safety and security that allows love to grow and flourish. Think of trust as a delicate flower, nurtured by the actions and words of both partners. It's built over time, like a beautiful garden that blooms with each loving gesture and honest conversation.

Think about it this way: trust is like a bridge between two souls, allowing them to cross over to a place of vulnerability and openness. It's earned through consistency and reliability, such as when promises are kept and commitments are honored. When you can count on someone, it creates a sense of comfort and security in the relationship.

And respect? It's like a dance of understanding and acceptance. Imagine that each partner has their own unique boundaries, opinions, and autonomy-their own space to be themselves. Respecting these differences is the key to a healthy and loving connection. Just as the sun and moon take turns shining in the sky, respect allows each partner to have their moments to shine and be heard.

In a relationship built on trust and respect, there is an openness to vulnerability and authenticity. It's a space where you can express your hopes and dreams without fear of judgment. Each partner is seen and heard, like stars twinkling brightly in the night sky, making the universe of love infinitely vast and wondrous.

During challenging times, trust and respect act as guiding stars, leading you to resolution and growth. Instead of pushing each other away, you come together, hand in hand, to navigate the rough waters, knowing that your bond is strong enough to weather any storm.

Do not forget that trust and respect are like delicate seeds that need nurturing and care. They grow with each act of kindness, forgiveness, and sincere effort to understand one another. As the garden of love blossoms with these pillars, your connection deepens into a bond that will stand the test of time.

Let's see trust and respect in action through a heartwarming example with dialogues:

Sophie and Liam have been dating for a few months. They're sitting in a cozy coffee shop, enjoying a cup of coffee together.

Sophie: (Looking a bit nervous) "Liam, there's something I've been meaning to talk to you about."

Liam: (Sincerely) "Of course, Sophie. You know you can talk to me about anything. What's on your mind?"

Sophie: "Well, I've noticed that sometimes you're not very punctual, and it's been bothering me a little. I feel anxious when you're late, and I start to worry that you won't show up."

Liam: (Listening attentively) "I appreciate you sharing that with me, Sophie. I'm sorry if my lateness has caused you any anxiety. It's not my intention to make you feel that way."

Sophie: "Thank you for understanding, Liam. It's just that being on time is important to me, and I value punctuality in my relationships."

Liam: "I completely understand, Sophie. I promise to work on being more punctual and respecting your time. Your feelings are important to me, and I want you to feel comfortable and secure when we make plans."

Sophie: (Smiling) "Thank you, Liam. That means a lot to me. I trust you, and I know you'll make an effort. It's just essential for us to communicate about these things."

Liam: "You're right. Communication is vital in any relationship. I want us to be open and honest with each other, so we can both feel valued and respected."

Sophie: (Feeling reassured) "I appreciate that, Liam. It makes me feel closer to you knowing that we can have these conversations without judgment."

Liam: "Absolutely, Sophie. I respect your feelings and your boundaries. We're a team, and we'll work together to make our relationship stronger."

In this dialogue, Sophie demonstrates emotional intimacy by expressing her feelings and concerns about Liam's lateness. She trusts Liam enough to share her vulnerability, and Liam responds with understanding and a willingness to change his behavior. Both partners communicate openly, showing respect for each other's feelings and boundaries.

As a result, their bond deepens, and they strengthen their relationship through trust and respect. This dialogue illustrates how trust and respect are essential in any loving relationship. It's through open communication and empathy that Sophie and Liam create a safe space for love to grow and flourish.

Communication

Think of communication as a wondrous magic wand that can transform the ordinary into the extraordinary. It's like a golden key that opens the doors to a treasure trove of understanding, empathy, and love. With this magical tool, you have the power to build bridges of connection that span the hearts of those you love.

But the real magic lies in active listening, the secret potion that enhances the magic of communication. It's not just nodding along or waiting for your turn to speak; it's being fully present in the moment, giving your undivided attention to the person speaking, and receiving their words with an open heart.

As you unlock this world of communication, you'll find your relationships blossoming like a garden in full bloom. The more you appreciate this art, the more bridges you build, creating a world of love, understanding and harmony.

So, dear reader, let's use this magic key to unlock the door to meaningful relationships. Through open and honest conversation and active listening with empathy, we'll cross those bridges with grace and compassion.

Let's see communication in action through an example with dialogues:

Alex and Sam have been in a relationship for a year. They're sitting on a park bench, enjoying the beautiful sunset together.

Alex: (Smiling) "Sam, I've been thinking about our future together, and there's something I'd like to discuss."

Sam: (Curious) "Sure, Alex. What's on your mind?"

Alex: "Well, I've been offered a job opportunity in a different city. It's a big step for my career, but it would mean being away from our families and friends."

Sam: (Attentive) "Oh, that's a significant decision, Alex. I'm glad you brought it up. Tell me more about the job and how you feel about it."

Alex: "The job itself is fantastic, and it's a great opportunity for me to grow professionally. But I'm torn because I don't want to be far from our support system and loved ones."

Sam: (Nods) "I understand, Alex. This is a big life change, and it's natural to have mixed feelings about it. I want you to know that I'm here to support you, no matter what you decide."

Alex: "Thank you, Sam. Your support means the world to me. I'm just afraid that if I choose the job, it might put a strain on our relationship."

Sam: "It's okay to be afraid, Alex. We can face this together. Let's talk about our options and find a solution that works for both of us."

Alex: (Feeling relieved) "You're right, Sam. We need to communicate openly about our feelings and concerns. I want us to make this decision together as a team."

Sam: "Absolutely, Alex. Our relationship is built on trust and communication. We'll navigate through this, and whatever happens, we'll face it together."

In this dialogue, Alex and Sam demonstrate the power of communication in their relationship. Alex opens up about the job opportunity and shares their thoughts and feelings with Sam. Sam responds with attentive listening and empathy, assuring Alex that they will face this decision together as a team.

Through their open and honest conversation, they build a bridge of understanding and support, strengthening their bond and creating a safe space for vulnerability. This dialogue shows how communication can foster trust, love, and connection in a relationship, even during challenging decisions and life changes.

Shared Values and Goals

Think of Shared Values and Goals as the strong foundation of a beautiful relationship. When you and your partner share similar values, it means that you both have a common understanding of what's important in life. It's like being on the same page, having a mutual agreement about what's most important to both of you. This shared understanding creates a sense of togetherness and alignment that makes you feel connected on a deeper level.

Having common goals is like having a common vision for your future. It's about supporting each other's dreams and aspirations, like two adventurers on a great quest together. When you cheer each other on, share the joys of success, and lift each other up when times are tough, it creates a powerful sense of partnership. You become a team that faces life's challenges hand-in-hand, knowing that you have a trusted ally by your side.

Shared values and goals in a relationship can vary from couple to couple, but here are a few examples to illustrate the concept:

- Family and together: Both partners prioritize family and togetherness as essential values. They share a goal of spending quality time with their extended family and creating traditions that strengthen their bonds with loved ones.

- Personal growth and learning: Both partners value personal growth and learning. They share a goal of supporting each other's pursuit of education, skill development, and self-improvement.

- Health and wellness: Both partners value their health and well-being. They have a shared goal of maintaining an active lifestyle, eating nutritious meals, and supporting each other in staying physically and mentally healthy.

- Financial responsibility: Both partners share the value of financial responsibility. They set goals to save money, avoid unnecessary debt, and make informed financial decisions together.

- Travel and Adventure: Both partners share a love of travel and adventure. They set a goal to explore new places together, experience different cultures, and create lasting memories through shared adventures.

- Giving back to the community: Both partners share the value of giving back to the community. They set a goal to volunteer or donate to charitable causes that are meaningful to them.

- Environmental awareness: Both partners share the value of caring for the environment and being aware of their carbon footprint. They set goals to reduce waste, use sustainable products, and make eco-friendly choices in their daily lives.

- Work-life balance: Both partners value work-life balance. They share a goal of supporting each other in achieving a healthy balance between their work and personal lives.

- Open communication and trust: Both partners value open communication and trust in their relationship. They have a shared goal of being honest and transparent with each other, creating a safe space for vulnerability and understanding.

- Long-term commitment: Both partners share the value of long-term commitment and building a life together. They have a shared goal of making decisions that contribute to the longevity and happiness of their relationship.

As you go on this adventure together, your bond deepens and your love grows stronger. It's like a unifying force that draws you closer together, creating a unique connection built on respect, understanding and support. Together, you create a world where your love shines like a beacon, guiding you to a bright and fulfilling future.

The Pillars of Love and Secure Attachment

Now that we've explored the four pillars of love, it's time to delve into an essential aspect that profoundly influences our ability to experience and nurture these pillars: secure attachment. Like the roots of a strong tree, secure attachment is the foundation of healthy and lasting relationships. It's like a loving hug that provides a sense of safety and comfort, allowing love to blossom and flourish.

But what is secure attachment? Well, picture it as the deep bond that forms between a child and his or her caregiver, usually a parent, in the early years of life. This attachment style lays the foundation for how we approach and connect with others in our adult relationships. When we have a secure attachment style, we bring trust, confidence, and emotional resilience to our relationships, making them all the more fulfilling and enriching.

To get a clearer understanding of insecure attachment styles, let's start with secure attachment. Secure attachment is the foundation of all other attachment styles, so it's important to understand it before we move on to the others. Once we have a good understanding of secure attachment, we can then explore the different insecure attachment styles and how they develop.

Secure Attachment Style

Secure attachment is an attachment style in the context of interpersonal relationships, primarily observed in parent-child relationships, but also applicable to other relationships throughout life. It is considered the most desirable and healthy attachment style, leading to positive emotional development and more satisfying interactions with others. Here's a breakdown of the key points about secure attachment:

People with a secure attachment style are comfortable with emotional intimacy and are confident in seeking support from others. They generally have a positive view of themselves and others, trusting that their needs will be met and that they can rely on their close relationships. They are able to express emotions and communicate openly without fear of rejection. These individuals tend to have a good balance between independence and the ability to connect with others.

Secure attachment is typically formed in early childhood through consistent and responsive caregiving. When parents or primary caregivers are sensitive to their child's needs and provide love, comfort, and reassurance in times of distress, the child learns that they can trust others to be there for them. This reliable support fosters a sense of security and provides a solid foundation for healthy relationships in the future.

Behavioral characteristics and distinguishing features:

- Emotional regulation: Securely attached individuals tend to have effective emotional regulation skills. They can manage their feelings and respond appropriately to emotional cues from others.

- Open Communication: They are comfortable expressing their needs and feelings and are receptive to the feelings and concerns of others.

- Comfortable with Intimacy: Secure individuals can engage in close, intimate relationships without feeling overwhelmed or overly dependent on others.

- Adaptability: They can adapt well to changes and challenges in relationships without feeling anxious or defensive.

- Empathy and compassion: Securely attached individuals show genuine concern and empathy for others, fostering positive and caring interactions.

Example

Let's consider an example of a person named Sarah with a secure attachment style. Throughout her childhood, Sarah's parents consistently provided emotional support, responded to her needs, and provided a safe base from which to explore the world. As a result, Sarah grew up feeling loved, valued, and confident in her relationships with others.

As an adult, Sarah maintains fulfilling and stable relationships. They are open and honest about their feelings and needs with their romantic partners, friends, and family. During times of stress or emotional challenge, Sarah seeks comfort and support from loved ones, knowing that they will be there to provide care and understanding. This ability to seek support and trust in her relationships makes Sarah feel emotionally secure, which increases her overall well-being and happiness. In addition, because of her secure attachment style, Sarah is also likely to show understanding and compassion to others when they need support, further strengthening her relationships.

It's important to note that while secure attachment is considered an ideal attachment style, individuals can develop different attachment patterns based on their early experiences. However, with awareness and effort, it's possible for individuals to work toward developing more secure and healthier attachment styles in adulthood.

Addressing Misconceptions

Misconception: People with secure attachments are always perfectly happy and have no relationship challenges.

Reality: While secure attachment is associated with healthier relationship patterns, it doesn't mean that people with a secure attachment style never experience difficulties or conflict in their relationships. They are simply better equipped to deal with challenges and are more likely to seek and provide support in times of stress.

Misconception: Secure attachment is solely a result of parenting and early childhood experiences.

Reality: While early caregiving plays a critical role in the development of attachment styles, it is not the only factor. Later experiences, such as supportive friendships or therapeutic relationships, can also influence and enhance secure attachment in adulthood.

Misconception: Secure attachment means complete independence and emotional self-sufficiency.

Reality: Secure attachment individuals value their relationships and emotional connections with others. While they are comfortable with themselves, they also value the support and closeness that comes with healthy, secure relationships.

Misconception: Only a small percentage of the population has a secure attachment style.

Reality: Secure attachment is a common and achievable attachment style. Many people develop secure attachment patterns through positive and nurturing experiences in their early years or through therapeutic interventions later in life.

Understanding these misconceptions about secure attachment can help us appreciate its importance and how it contributes to healthier and more fulfilling relationships. It also emphasizes the potential for growth and positive change in attachment styles, so that individuals can work toward developing more secure patterns even if they didn't experience secure attachment in their early years.

In the world of relationships, love is like a puzzle with many pieces. The main pillars of love – emotional intimacy, trust and respect, communication, and shared values and goals – are the foundation that holds healthy and fulfilling connections together. By understanding and nurturing these pillars, we can create a loving and harmonious bond with those we care about.

Now, let's explore the fascinating realm of insecure attachment, beginning with anxious attachment. Discover how our early experiences shape our approach to love and intimacy, and learn how understanding and transforming these attachment styles can lead to more meaningful and lasting relationships.

Chapter 4: Anxious Attachment

Why do some individuals in romantic relationships constantly seek reassurance and fear rejection or abandonment?

Anxious attachment is one of the three insecure attachment styles and typically develops in early childhood. It often results from inappropriate and inconsistent parenting, leading to feelings of insecurity and a strong fear of rejection or abandonment in close relationships. People with an anxious attachment style may show signs of low self-esteem and clinginess in their relationships, seeking constant reassurance and validation from their partners.

This attachment style can have lasting effects on adult relationships, affecting the way individuals relate to their romantic partners. It is associated with an increased need for intimacy combined with doubt and fear of abandonment. Relationships with anxious adults may involve both a desire for closeness and a fear of rejection, leading to emotional ups and downs.

Anxious attachment is a relatively common attachment style among adults, with a significant portion of the population experiencing varying degrees of these tendencies in their romantic relationships. Research suggests that about 20% of people have an anxious attachment style.

Children who grow up with inconsistent or unpredictable caregiving, where their emotional needs are not consistently met, may be more likely to develop anxious attachment tendencies in their adult relationships. For example, a child whose caregiver is sometimes responsive and attentive, but at other times distant or unresponsive, may learn to be hyper-vigilant and anxious about the availability of love and care.

In such cases, the child may develop a heightened need for closeness and reassurance from romantic partners, fearing rejection or abandonment because of past experiences of emotional unavailability. This early attachment pattern, if not addressed or resolved, can persist into adulthood and influence how individuals bond and relate in their romantic relationships.

People with anxious attachment may have certain identifiable characteristics:

Excessive need for reassurance

Anxiously attached individuals have an intense need for emotional reassurance from their partners. They constantly seek verbal affirmations, gestures of love, and expressions of commitment to feel safe and valued in the relationship. They may repeatedly ask their partner if they love them, need constant reminders of their partner's feelings, and seek validation of their worthiness in the relationship. Despite receiving reassurance, their fears may resurface, leading to a never-ending cycle of seeking more reassurance.

Fear of abandonment

Anxiously attached individuals carry deep-seated fears of being abandoned or left alone. They may have experienced inconsistent caregiving in childhood, which left them feeling insecure and uncertain about their relationships. As a result, they are hypersensitive to any signs of distance from their partner, such as delayed responses to messages or a decrease in affectionate behavior. These small cues can trigger intense anxiety, leading them to question the stability of the relationship and fear that their partner may leave them.

Overthinking and sensitivity

Anxious attachers tend to overanalyze every interaction with their partner. They scrutinize conversations, actions, and even nonverbal cues, trying to decipher their partner's true feelings and intentions. Innocent comments or gestures may be misinterpreted as signs of rejection or disinterest, fueling their insecurities. Their heightened sensitivity to emotional cues can lead to a pattern of reading into situations that may have no underlying issues.

Jealousy and possessiveness

Because of their deep-seated fear of losing their partner's affection and attention, anxiously attached individuals may struggle with jealousy and possessiveness. They may become overly vigilant about potential threats to the relationship and feel threatened by their partner's interactions with others. This jealousy stems from their intense need for emotional security and fear of being replaced or overlooked.

Emotional roller coaster

Anxiously attached individuals often experience emotional highs and lows based on their perception of the stability of the relationship. When they feel secure and loved, they may experience moments of joy and satisfaction. However, even minor doubts or uncertainties can quickly plunge them into feelings of anxiety, sadness, and self-doubt. These emotional fluctuations can create an unpredictable atmosphere in the relationship and contribute to communication challenges.

Formation of Anxious Attachment in Childhood

Parents or caregivers can inadvertently contribute to the development of anxious attachment in children through certain behaviors and interactions. It's important to note that most parents have good intentions and may not be aware of the impact their actions can have on their child's attachment style. Here are some ways that parental behaviors can lead to anxious attachment:

Inconsistent responsiveness

When caregivers are inconsistent in responding to a child's emotional needs, the child may experience confusion and uncertainty in his or her interactions with the caregiver. For example, when the child seeks comfort or reassurance in times of distress, sometimes the caregiver may be empathetic and reassuring, providing a secure emotional base for the child. At other times, however, the caregiver may be dismissive, unavailable, or preoccupied with his or her own concerns, leaving the child feeling ignored, rejected, or invalidated. This inconsistency can cause the child to develop a hyper-vigilant and anxious response to the caregiver's behavior, never knowing what to expect in times of emotional need. As a result, the child may constantly seek the caregiver's closeness and attention to alleviate his or her anxiety and insecurity.

Overprotectiveness

Overprotective parents may have good intentions in trying to keep their child safe. However, overprotection can inhibit the child's exploration and independence, causing the child to become overly dependent on the caregiver. When parents limit a child's opportunities for age-appropriate risk-taking and learning from experiences, the child may feel anxious and uncertain about his or her own abilities and decision-making skills. This anxiety may manifest as a reluctance to explore new situations, seek autonomy, or interact independently with others because the child has learned to rely heavily on the caregiver's guidance and intervention.

Intrusiveness

Parents who are overly intrusive or controlling may interfere with the child's personal boundaries and autonomy, creating a sense of emotional suffocation. For example, a parent may constantly invade the child's personal space, emotions, or friendships, not allowing the child to have private thoughts or feelings. The child may feel overwhelmed by the constant intrusion and unable to develop a sense of self and independence. As a result, the child may become anxious and reluctant to express himself or herself openly, fearing possible negative reactions from the caregiver.

Emotional neglect

Emotional neglect occurs when a caregiver consistently fails to acknowledge or respond to a child's emotional needs. This may include dismissing the child's feelings, ignoring his or her emotional distress, or failing to provide comfort and support in times of need. Emotional neglect can make the child feel unimportant and insignificant, leading to a sense of isolation and fear of seeking emotional support from others. The child may internalize the message that their feelings are unimportant or unworthy of attention, making them reluctant to express their feelings and needs to others.

Overly critical or rejecting

When parents are overly critical or frequently reject the child's actions, behaviors, or emotions, the child may internalize a sense of unworthiness and self-doubt. Constant criticism can create a pervasive sense of being flawed or unlovable, leading the child to develop a heightened sense of anxiety and a constant need for validation and approval. The child may engage in people-pleasing behaviors in an attempt to gain acceptance and avoid rejection from caregivers, friends, or authority figures.

Parental anxiety

Parents who experience high levels of anxiety may inadvertently transfer their own anxiety to the child. Children are sensitive to their caregivers' emotions, and if they sense their caregiver's anxiety, they may interpret it as a signal of potential danger or threat. This can cause the child to become anxious and vigilant about his or her environment, constantly looking for signs of danger or harm. The child may also internalize the caregiver's anxiety, experiencing chronic worry and fear even in situations that may not warrant such a response.

Role reversal

In certain family dynamics, parents may rely on their child for emotional support or treat the child as a confidant or surrogate partner. This role reversal can create a burdensome and inappropriate emotional responsibility for the child, leading to feelings of anxiety, overwhelm, and inadequacy. The child may have difficulty distinguishing his or her own needs from those of the caregiver and may sacrifice his or her emotional well-being to meet the caregiver's emotional demands. As a result, the child may experience anxiety about his or her own emotional needs and have difficulty establishing healthy boundaries in future relationships.

Unresolved trauma

Parents who have unresolved trauma or attachment issues from their own childhood may find it difficult to provide a secure emotional base for their child. Unresolved trauma can interfere with the parent's ability to be emotionally present and attuned to their child's needs, as they may be preoccupied with their own emotional struggles. As a result, the child may feel emotionally neglected or disconnected from the caregiver, leading to anxious attachment behaviors such as seeking constant validation or attention to compensate for the perceived emotional absence.

It's essential to keep in mind that no parent is perfect, and occasional lapses in responsiveness or mistakes are normal. The development of attachment styles is a complex interplay of various factors, and it's not determined by any single action or behavior of the parent. In addition, children may have different temperaments and sensitivities that influence how they respond to parenting behaviors.

Example

Meet Alex. Growing up, Alex's parents were often preoccupied with their busy careers, leaving little time for emotional connection with him. As a child, Alex longed for his parents' attention and affection, but it seemed elusive, leading to a sense of emotional insecurity. As an adult with an anxious attachment style, Alex finds himself in constant turmoil in his relationships. He craves intimacy and closeness, but the fear of rejection and abandonment haunts him, causing him to become overly clingy and anxious. His need for reassurance often strains his relationships, as his partners feel overwhelmed and stifled by his constant need for validation.

Here are some common words and phrases that people with anxious attachment may use:

1. "Always" and "never": They might use these absolute terms when expressing fears or concerns about their partner's behavior, such as "You never call me when you're away" or "You always seem distant."

2. "Do you love me?": People with anxious attachment may frequently seek validation of their partner's feelings and affection, often asking direct questions about their love and commitment.

3. "What if...": Anxious individuals may engage in catastrophic thinking and express concerns about negative outcomes in the relationship, using phrases like "What if you stop loving me?" or "What if you find someone better?"

4. "I'm sorry": They may apologize excessively, even for minor things, to

avoid conflict and maintain the connection with their partner.

5. "Are you mad at me?": Anxious individuals may be hypersensitive to any perceived changes in their partner's behavior and seek immediate reassurance to dispel any doubts about their partner's feelings.

6. "Please don't leave me": Fear of abandonment is a core aspect of anxious attachment, leading individuals to express their fear of losing their partner.

7. "I can't live without you": Anxious individuals may express intense dependency on their partner, believing their emotional well-being is solely reliant on the relationship.

8. "You didn't reply...": They may become distressed or anxious if their partner takes longer to respond to messages, interpreting it as a sign of rejection or disinterest.

9. "Are you sure you want to be with me?": Seeking constant reassurance about the relationship's stability and their partner's commitment is common for people with anxious attachment.

10. "I'm just being silly": To downplay their anxieties, they may dismiss their feelings as irrational or unwarranted, even when their fears are rooted in genuine concerns.

Romantic relationships can be incredibly rewarding and fulfilling, but they also come with challenges. Here are some of the most common challenges that partners may face:

Anxiously attached individuals may be hyper-vigilant in detecting signs of potential rejection or disinterest on the part of their partner. For example, if their partner is busy with work or social commitments, they may interpret this as a lack of interest in the relationship rather than recognizing the external factors at play. This misinterpretation can lead to unnecessary conflict, as the anxiously attached person seeks reassurance and validation, while their partner may feel unfairly accused or misunderstood.

Feeling smothered or suffocated

Anxiously attached people's constant need for reassurance and emotional closeness can cause their partners to feel overwhelmed and suffocated. For example, if the anxious person insists on frequent check-ins throughout the day or becomes overly possessive, the partner may feel trapped or controlled. This dynamic can strain the relationship, as the partner may desire more personal space and independence, creating tension between his or her need for autonomy and the anxiously attached person's need for constant connection.

Unresolved conflicts

Communication challenges in relationships with anxiously attached individuals can impede conflict resolution. When conflict arises, anxiously attached individuals may have difficulty expressing their feelings clearly and openly. Instead, they may resort to passive-aggressive behavior or emotional withdrawal, making it difficult for their partner to fully understand their needs. As a result, conflicts may linger and remain unresolved, leading to increased emotional distance between partners and potential resentment over time.

Partner feels inadequate

Anxiously attached individuals' deep-seated insecurities can inadvertently make their partners feel inadequate or as if they can never fully meet their emotional needs. For example, if the anxious person constantly seeks validation and reassurance of his or her partner's love and commitment, the partner may begin to question his or her ability to adequately meet these needs. This dynamic can lead to frustration and a sense of helplessness in the partner, who may feel unable to meet the insatiable emotional demands of the anxiously attached person.

Emotional exhaustion

Riding the emotional roller coaster of an anxiously attached partner can be emotionally draining for the significant other. The anxiously attached person may experience frequent mood swings, seeking constant reassurance one moment and withdrawing emotionally the next. Their partner may find it difficult to keep up with these rapidly changing emotions, leading to feelings of exhaustion and burnout. This emotional exhaustion can interfere with the partner's ability to meet his or her own emotional needs and create a sense of imbalance in the relationship.

Address misconceptions

Misconception: Anxious people are overly clingy and dependent in relationships.

Reality: While individuals with anxious attachment may seek closeness and reassurance, this doesn't mean they are overly dependent. Their deep longing for intimacy is often rooted in early experiences that have shaped their attachment style, making them more sensitive to changes in their relationships.

Misconception: Anxious attachment is a sign of neediness or insecurity.

Reality: Anxious attachment is a natural response to inconsistent caregiving during childhood. It doesn't reflect weakness or inadequacy, but rather a genuine need for emotional support and a strong desire for a secure and loving connection.

Misconception: Anxious people are always anxious and unhappy in relationships.

Reality: While anxious individuals may experience periods of heightened anxiety in relationships, they are also capable of experiencing joy, love, and happiness. Their emotional intensity and fear of abandonment do not negate their capacity for positive emotions and meaningful relationships.

Misconception: Anxious attachment is a personality flaw that cannot be changed.

Reality: Like all attachment styles, anxious attachment can be influenced and changed over time. With self-awareness, introspection, and support from therapy or healthy relationships, individuals with anxious attachment can develop more secure attachment patterns and foster greater emotional security.

Misconception: Anxious individuals are overly demanding and need constant reassurance.

Reality: Anxious individuals seek reassurance because they fear rejection and value the emotional connection in their relationships. They can benefit from open communication and understanding partners who can help create a safe emotional environment.

In short, understanding anxious attachment is crucial to understanding the emotional dynamics that influence our romantic relationships. This attachment style, formed in response to inconsistent care during childhood, can lead individuals to desire intimacy while harboring deep fears of rejection and abandonment. The need for reassurance and validation can lead to emotional ups and downs that affect the quality and stability of relationships.

Recognizing the characteristics and language associated with anxious attachment helps us empathize with and support people with this attachment style. It also allows us to foster healthier attachments by providing the emotional reassurance and security they seek.

In the next chapter, we will explore avoidant attachment, another piece of the attachment puzzle. Exploring avoidant attachment will shed further light on how early experiences shape our adult behavior in relationships.

Chapter 5: Avoidant Attachment

Have you ever wondered why some people seem to avoid seeking comfort and support from others, even in difficult times? How does this unique attachment style affect their ability to form meaningful bonds with others, including romantic relationships and friendships?

Avoidant attachment, one of the three insecure attachment styles described in psychological theory, represents a unique reluctance to seek comfort and support from others, even in times of distress. Those who embody this attachment style often downplay the value of close relationships and struggle with emotional intimacy.

The impact of avoidant attachment on the population is widespread and profound. Emerging research suggests that individuals with avoidant tendencies have difficulty forming and maintaining meaningful connections with others. These challenges manifest not only in their romantic endeavors, but also permeate their friendships and even professional interactions. Understanding the intricacies of avoidant attachment is essential to unlocking healthier relationship dynamics and fostering emotional well-being.

Avoidant attachment manifests itself in observable patterns of behavior and emotional responses. Some key characteristics of individuals with avoidant attachment include:

Emotional Independence

Individuals with avoidant attachment tend to place a high value on emotional independence. They may have learned from early experiences that relying on others for emotional support can lead to disappointment or vulnerability. As a result, they may become self-reliant and minimize the importance of seeking help or comfort from others. This emotional independence can sometimes be mistaken for emotional strength, as they may appear stoic and composed even in difficult situations. However, this tendency to suppress emotions and avoid seeking support can have negative consequences, leading to feelings of isolation and loneliness.

Fear of intimacy

Intimacy involves emotional closeness, vulnerability, and sharing one's inner thoughts and feelings with another person. For people with avoidant attachment, the idea of emotional intimacy can be frightening. They may have learned early on that emotional dependence on others can lead to rejection or harm. As a result, they may avoid deep emotional relationships or be uncomfortable with displays of affection. This fear of intimacy can be a barrier to forming meaningful relationships and can lead to a cycle of distancing oneself from others in order to protect oneself from potential emotional pain.

Difficulty trusting others

Trust is a fundamental aspect of any healthy relationship. However, individuals with avoidant attachment may have difficulty trusting others fully. Their early experiences may have taught them that depending on others is risky and may not result in reliable support. As a result, they may have difficulty believing that others will be there for them when they need them. This lack of trust can make it difficult for them to open up and share their emotions with others, further reinforcing their independent tendencies.

Dismissing emotions

In response to distress or uncomfortable emotions, individuals with avoidant attachment may dismiss or suppress their feelings. This may be a coping mechanism developed in childhood to avoid feeling overwhelmed or helpless. By minimizing their emotions, they may be trying to regain a sense of control and independence. However, denying emotions can hinder emotional growth and interpersonal communication. It can also lead to a lack of emotional awareness, making it difficult for them to effectively identify and address their emotional needs.

Preference for independence

Independence is valued by individuals with avoidant attachment, and they may prioritize personal space and autonomy in their relationships. While independence is a healthy aspect of any relationship, an excessive focus on it can lead to emotional distance from others. They may be uncomfortable with emotional dependence on their partners, friends, or family members and may prefer to deal with their problems on their own. This preference for independence can create challenges in forming and maintaining close, supportive relationships with others.

Formation of Avoidant Attachment in Childhood

Avoidant attachment typically develops in early childhood based on interactions with primary caregivers, particularly during infancy. The primary factors that contribute to the formation of avoidant attachment include:

Caregiver Responsiveness

The formation of avoidant attachment in childhood is strongly influenced by caregiver responsiveness. When caregivers are consistently responsive to an infant's needs, they create a safe and nurturing environment. Responsive caregivers respond promptly to the child's cues for comfort, food, and affection, which fosters a sense of trust and safety in the child. As a result, the child develops a secure attachment style, which is characterized by a positive view of self and others.

Emotional availability

Emotionally available caregivers are attuned to the child's emotional cues and respond with warmth and empathy. When a child expresses distress or happiness, emotionally available caregivers acknowledge and validate these feelings. This emotional validation helps the child develop emotional regulation skills and a positive self-image. Emotionally available caregivers also provide a safe space for the child to explore and express his or her emotions without fear of rejection or judgment.

Inconsistent responses

Avoidant attachment can develop when caregivers are inconsistent or unresponsive to the child's emotional cues. If caregivers are sometimes available and supportive, but at other times neglectful or dismissive of the child's emotions, the child may develop a coping strategy of emotional withdrawal. In such cases, the child may learn that seeking emotional support is unpredictable, leading him or her to suppress emotions and avoid seeking help.

Parental rejection

In extreme cases, avoidant attachment can result from parental rejection or neglect. If caregivers repeatedly reject a child's requests for emotional connection or fail to meet his or her emotional needs, the child may internalize a sense of worthlessness and develop a defensive strategy of emotional withdrawal. This coping mechanism helps the child avoid the pain of rejection, but can have long-term consequences for his or her ability to trust and connect with others.

Overemphasis on independence

In some families, caregivers may overemphasize independence and discourage emotional expression or dependency. They may encourage self-reliance and devalue emotional vulnerability, inadvertently influencing the development of an avoidant attachment style in the child. Such parenting practices may hinder the child's emotional development and create challenges in forming intimate relationships later in life.

Example

Let's consider Lily, who has an avoidant attachment style. During childhood, Lily's parents were often preoccupied with their own lives, leaving Lily to deal with her emotions alone. Whenever Lily expressed vulnerability or sadness, his parents dismissed his feelings and encouraged him to be strong and independent. As an adult, Lily finds it challenging to open up emotionally to his romantic partners. He downplays the importance of emotional intimacy, preferring to focus on the practical aspects of the relationship and avoiding conversations about deeper feelings. When faced with conflict or emotional challenges, Lily withdraws emotionally, leaving his partner feeling excluded and unimportant.

People with avoidant attachment tend to use words and phrases that reflect emotional distance, self-reliance, and a preference for independence. Some common words and phrases they may use include:

> 1. "I'm fine." - Avoidant individuals often downplay their emotions and may use this phrase to dismiss or avoid discussing their feelings.

2. "I don't need anyone." - They may emphasize their self-sufficiency and independence, suggesting that they can handle their emotions on their own.

3. "I prefer to deal with things alone." - Avoidant individuals may express a preference for handling their problems and emotions without seeking help or support from others.

4. "I don't like getting too close to people." - They may verbalize a reluctance to form deep emotional connections or intimate relationships.

5. "I value my personal space." - Avoidant individuals may emphasize the importance of having boundaries and personal space in their relationships.

6. "I'm not the emotional type." - They may distance themselves from emotions and avoid expressing vulnerability.

7. "It's better not to rely on others." - Avoidant individuals may express a belief that depending on others can lead to disappointment or vulnerability.

8. "I don't like talking about feelings." - They may avoid conversations that involve emotional depth or vulnerability.

9. "I don't want to burden anyone with my problems." - Avoidant individuals may feel hesitant to share their emotions with others, believing it could be burdensome for those around them.

10. "I'd rather be alone." - They may express a preference for solitude or time spent by themselves.

Romantic relationships can be incredibly rewarding and fulfilling, but they also come with their fair share of challenges. Some of the common challenges that partners in a romantic relationship may face include:

Communication issues

Effective communication is the cornerstone of a healthy relationship. However, partners often encounter barriers when trying to communicate openly and honestly. Communication problems can arise from a variety of factors, such as different communication styles, fear of confrontation, or past experiences that have shaped the way partners express themselves. Poor communication can lead to misunderstandings, unresolved conflicts, and emotional distance between partners. To overcome communication challenges, couples can work on active listening, clearly expressing their needs and feelings, and practicing empathy to understand each other's perspectives.

Emotional intimacy

Emotional intimacy involves sharing one's innermost thoughts, feelings, and vulnerabilities with a partner. It requires trust and a willingness to be emotionally open. Some partners may find it difficult to be vulnerable because of past experiences of emotional hurt or fear of being judged or rejected. A lack of emotional intimacy can lead to feelings of disconnection and isolation in the relationship. Building emotional intimacy requires creating a safe and non-judgmental space where both partners can express themselves freely and honestly.

Conflict and Disagreement

All couples experience disagreement and conflict from time to time. Conflict can result from differences in opinions, values, and expectations. How partners handle conflict is critical to the health of the relationship. Avoiding conflict or engaging in harmful communication patterns, such as criticism and defensiveness, can escalate the situation. Constructive conflict resolution involves active listening, empathy, compromise, and a focus on finding solutions that meet the needs of both partners.

Trust issues

Trust is the foundation of any strong relationship. However, past experiences of betrayal, dishonesty, or unresolved conflict can lead to trust issues in a romantic partnership. Rebuilding trust takes time, consistency, and open communication. Both partners must be willing to be transparent, reliable, and understanding as they work through trust issues together.

Differences in expectations

Partners may enter a relationship with different expectations about various aspects of their life together. These expectations may include plans for the future, career aspirations, desired living arrangements, or even the level of emotional closeness. It is important for partners to have open discussions about their expectations and work to find common ground and compromise where necessary.

Balancing independence and togetherness

Maintaining a balance between individuality and togetherness can be challenging. Some partners may struggle to find the right balance, leading to feelings of suffocation or neglect. Healthy relationships allow each partner to maintain individual interests, hobbies, and friendships while nurturing their connection as a couple. Effective communication about personal boundaries and needs is key to achieving this balance.

Life transitions

Major life transitions, such as moving to a new city, starting a new job, or experiencing the loss of a loved one, can affect the relationship. These changes can bring additional stress and uncertainty that can affect how partners interact and support each other. During life transitions, partners need to communicate openly, be patient with each other's emotions, and offer understanding and support.

Intimacy and sexual issues

Intimacy and sexual dynamics in a relationship may change over time. Physical and emotional factors, stress, and medical conditions can affect sexual desire and satisfaction. Open and compassionate communication is critical to addressing these issues. Seeking professional help from a sex therapist or counselor may also be beneficial.

Time Management

Balancing personal, work, and relationship responsibilities can be challenging. Time management challenges can leave partners feeling neglected or overwhelmed. It is important to prioritize quality time together and support each other in managing their respective responsibilities.

External stressors

External stressors, such as financial difficulties, work-related stress, or family conflict, can affect the dynamics of the relationship. Partners need to support each other during difficult times and find healthy ways to cope with stress together.

Long-distance relationships

Couples in long-distance relationships face the added challenge of physical separation. Maintaining emotional closeness and trust despite distance requires effective communication, regular visits, and a shared vision for the future.

Past baggage

Everyone brings past experiences and emotional baggage to a relationship. Unresolved issues from past relationships or childhood can affect current relationships. Partners should be understanding and supportive and help each other address and heal from past wounds.

Lack of quality time

Finding quality time to connect and bond can be difficult, especially in today's busy lifestyles. Making time for regular date nights or activities that both partners enjoy can help strengthen the emotional bond.

Financial Disagreements

Disagreements about money and financial priorities can strain a relationship. Partners should have open discussions about financial goals, budgeting, and how they will manage finances together.

External interference

Outside influences, such as family members or friends, can interfere with the relationship. Partners need to communicate boundaries and prioritize their relationship, while handling outside interference with tact and respect.

Address misconceptions

Misconception: Avoidant people don't want close relationships.

Reality: While avoidant individuals may appear aloof, they still desire connection and intimacy. However, their early experiences have taught them to suppress their emotions and be independent, making it difficult for them to openly express their needs and feelings.

Misconception: Avoidant attachment is a sign of emotional unavailability or commitment phobia.

Reality: Avoidant attachment is a learned coping mechanism, not a conscious choice to be emotionally distant. Individuals with this style often fear emotional vulnerability and may have difficulty expressing their feelings, but this doesn't mean they are incapable of emotional connection.

Misconception: Avoidant people don't experience pain or hurt in relationships.

Reality: Avoidant individuals can experience emotional pain just like anyone else. However, they may internalize their feelings and deal with them privately rather than seeking support from others.

Misconception: Avoidant styles cannot change.

Reality: While attachment styles are formed early in life, they can be influenced by later experiences and personal growth. With self-awareness and therapeutic support, individuals with an avoidant attachment style can develop more secure attachment patterns and cultivate healthier relationships.

Avoidant attachment is a complex attachment style that can make it difficult to form meaningful connections.

People with avoidant attachment styles tend to be emotionally independent, fear intimacy, and have difficulty trusting others. They may also dismiss their emotions. Early experiences with caregivers play a significant role in the formation of avoidant attachment.

The next chapter will discuss disorganized attachment, a unique and challenging attachment style.

Disorganized attachment is characterized by conflicting behaviors and emotions. People with disorganized attachment styles may experience fear, anger, and sadness at the same time. They may also have difficulty trusting others and may feel like they are not worthy of love.

Understanding disorganized attachment can help us address unresolved trauma and foster healthier relationships.

Chapter 6: Disorganized Attachment

Have you ever encountered an attachment style that seems to defy categorization, with individuals oscillating between seeking closeness and avoiding emotional connections altogether?

Disorganized attachment represents a multifaceted and fascinating attachment style characterized by an absence of coherent behavioral strategies toward caregivers. Individuals with disorganized attachment exhibit a confusing interplay of inconsistent and contradictory responses to caregivers, vacillating between seeking comfort and withdrawing altogether. This attachment style reveals confused and occasionally anxious behaviors when confronted with distressing situations, leaving them uncertain about seeking support or protection.

Disorganized attachment is a complex and enigmatic attachment style that differs from the more clearly defined styles of secure, avoidant, or anxious attachment. Unlike other styles, disorganized attachment defies easy categorization because it includes elements of both avoidance and anxiety in relationships.

Disorganized attachment is expressed in observable patterns of behavior and emotional responses. Some key characteristics of individuals with disorganized attachment include:

Conflicting behaviors

Individuals with disorganized attachment often exhibit a confusing mix of contradictory behaviors, leaving caregivers and observers puzzled. At one moment, they may reach out to their caregivers for comfort and closeness, demonstrating a genuine desire for emotional connection. Just as quickly, however, they may withdraw, avoiding their caregivers and creating distance. This back-and-forth pattern of approach and avoidance can make it difficult for others to respond appropriately, perpetuating the cycle of confusion in their relationships.

Anxious and confused reactions

One of the defining characteristics of disorganized attachment is the expression of anxious and confused reactions, especially in response to stressful situations or attachment-related stressors. When faced with emotionally charged moments, individuals with disorganized attachment may appear disoriented and overwhelmed. Their emotions seem to pull them in conflicting directions, leaving them uncertain about how to seek support or protection from their attachment figures.

Unresolved trauma

The roots of disorganized attachment can often be traced to early experiences of unresolved trauma or frightening interactions with caregivers. These traumatic events may include experiences of abuse, neglect, or exposure to distressing circumstances without adequate support. As a result, individuals with disorganized attachment develop a complex mixture of longing for emotional closeness and fear of potential harm or rejection from their caregivers.

Disrupted caregiving environment

In some cases, disorganized attachment results from inconsistent or disorganized caregiving during early childhood. Caregivers who are struggling with unresolved trauma, grief, or mental health issues may inadvertently project their emotional turmoil onto the child. The lack of predictability and safety in the child's interactions with caregivers can disrupt the development of a secure internal working model of attachment.

Lack of a secure internal working model

Secure attachment is based on a coherent and organized internal working model, a mental framework that helps individuals understand and navigate relationships. However, individuals with disorganized attachment lack this secure internal model, which typically guides their emotional regulation and strategies for seeking support from others. The lack of a reliable roadmap for emotional security and connection contributes to their inconsistent behavior and emotional responses in relationships.

Formation of Disorganized Attachment in Childhood

Several critical factors contribute to the formation of disorganized attachment, each of which has a lasting impact on the child's emotional development:

The caregiver's role in the trauma

In some cases, the caregiver becomes the source of trauma or fear for the child. This distressing scenario results from abusive or neglectful behaviors on the part of the caregiver who inadvertently becomes both a source of comfort and a source of fear for the child. The child is caught in a confusing loop of seeking closeness and security from the same person who instills fear and insecurity.

Unresolved grief

Loss or separation from a primary caregiver can trigger unresolved grief in the child. The lack of adequate emotional processing and support during such distressing experiences can lead to disorganized attachment behaviors. The child may struggle to manage his or her emotions effectively, oscillating between seeking comfort and withdrawing as he or she comes to terms with the absence of the caregiver.

Inconsistent responses

When caregivers respond to the child's distress with unpredictability or disorganization, the child's attachment system becomes confused. Confused about how to seek support and comfort, the child may develop a disorganized pattern of behavior. This inconsistency in caregiver responses leaves the child uncertain about whether caregivers can be relied upon in times of need.

Traumatic events

Experiencing or witnessing traumatic events without adequate support and comfort from caregivers can significantly impact attachment formation. When faced with distressing situations, the child may lack a secure base to turn to for protection and reassurance. This lack of reliable support can lead to feelings of helplessness and a subsequent disorganized attachment style.

Parental Mental Health

The mental health of caregivers plays a critical role in shaping a child's attachment style. If caregivers are struggling with their own mental health issues or unresolved trauma, they may have difficulty providing consistent and supportive care to the child. The resulting instability and emotional turbulence in the caregiving environment contributes to disorganized attachment patterns in the child.

People with disorganized attachment may use words that reflect their conflicted and disoriented emotional experiences. Some common words and phrases they may use include:

1. I don't really know what I want." - Individuals with disorganized attachment may express uncertainty about their desires and needs, as they struggle with conflicting emotions and reactions.

2. "I feel like I'm always on edge." - They may describe feeling constantly anxious or on guard, unable to relax in relationships due to their past experiences.

3. "I can't trust anyone completely." - Disorganized individuals may express a lack of trust in others, stemming from their experiences of inconsistent caregiving and difficulty relying on others for support.

4. "I push people away, but I don't want to be alone." - They may acknowledge a pattern of pushing others away as a defense mechanism, while simultaneously desiring emotional connection and intimacy.

5. "I have a hard time making sense of my emotions." - Disorganized individuals may verbalize their struggles in understanding and managing their emotions, as they often experience conflicting and overwhelming feelings.

6. "I feel drawn to and scared of intimacy at the same time." - They may describe a paradoxical pull towards intimacy and fear of emotional vulnerability in relationships.

7. "I don't know how to handle conflicts." - Disorganized attachment can lead to challenges in dealing with conflicts or disagreements in a relationship, as they may be unsure how to navigate emotional interactions.

8. "I sometimes feel disconnected from myself." - They may express feelings of disconnection or detachment from their emotions and sense of self, reflecting the internal conflicts they experience.

9. "I have difficulty setting boundaries." - Disorganized individuals may struggle to establish clear boundaries in relationships, which can lead to challenges in maintaining healthy connections.

10. "I have a hard time trusting my instincts." - They may express doubts about their ability to trust their own judgment and decision-making, given their confusing emotional experiences.

These phrases reflect the complex and often contradictory emotions experienced by individuals with disorganized attachment. It is essential to approach them with sensitivity and understanding, as they navigate their unique challenges in forming and maintaining meaningful relationships.

Example

Consider Jake, who has a disorganized attachment style. In his childhood, Jake experienced periods of neglect and emotional abuse at the hands of his parents. At times they would show affection, but at other times they would lash out in anger. As a result, Jake's emotional responses became disorganized and unpredictable. In his adult relationships, Jake struggles to feel secure and often vacillates between desperately seeking emotional closeness and pushing his partner away when he feels overwhelmed. His fear of rejection and emotional volatility create a sense of chaos in his relationships, making it difficult to form lasting bonds.

Partners in a romantic relationship in which one person is experiencing disorganized attachment may face a number of unique challenges that stem from the complexities of this attachment style. Some of the challenges they may face are:

Conflicting behaviors

The partner with disorganized attachment may exhibit contradictory behaviors that can be confusing and destabilizing for their partner. One moment they may seek emotional closeness and intimacy, expressing a desire for connection and support. However, without warning, they may abruptly withdraw or become emotionally distant, leaving their partner feeling insecure and unsure of their true intentions.

Emotional distance

Individuals with disorganized attachment may struggle with emotional intimacy and have difficulty expressing their feelings. Their fear of vulnerability and past experiences of emotional hurt may cause them to put up emotional walls, making it difficult for their partner to get to know them on a deeper emotional level.

Fear of abandonment

Disorganized attachment often involves a deep-seated fear of abandonment resulting from unresolved attachment issues. The partner with disorganized attachment may experience intense fear that their partner will leave or reject them, resulting in a constant need for reassurance and validation.

Difficulty trusting

Trust is a fundamental element of any healthy relationship, but for someone with disorganized attachment, trust can be a significant hurdle. Past experiences of inconsistent care or traumatic events can create a deep sense of suspicion, making it difficult for them to fully trust their partner's intentions and reliability.

Unpredictable reactions

Partners may find it difficult to predict how their loved one with disorganized attachment will react to certain situations or triggers. The partner's emotional responses may seem erratic and volatile, leading to confusion and uncertainty in the relationship.

Fear of emotional vulnerability

Expressing vulnerability and seeking emotional support may be difficult for the partner with disorganized attachment. They may have learned early on that showing vulnerability makes them vulnerable to pain or rejection, so they avoid emotional openness.

Communication issues

Effective communication is the cornerstone of a thriving relationship, but disorganized attachment can interfere with clear and constructive communication. The partner with disorganized attachment may have difficulty expressing their needs, feelings, and expectations, leading to misunderstandings and unresolved conflicts.

Attachment-related conflicts

Conflicts in the relationship may often revolve around attachment-related issues such as emotional distance, fear of abandonment, or the need for reassurance. These conflicts can be particularly difficult to resolve because of the underlying attachment dynamics at play.

Emotional triggers

Certain situations or behaviors by the partner may inadvertently trigger past traumas or unresolved emotions in the disorganized attachment partner. As a result, their emotional reactions may be heightened, adding complexity to managing relationship dynamics.

Feeling misunderstood

The disorganized attachment partner may feel misunderstood or isolated in their emotional experiences. Their struggle to effectively communicate their needs and feelings can lead to a sense of disconnection and loneliness.

Inconsistent support

Providing consistent emotional support to a partner with disorganized attachment can be challenging. They may find it difficult to provide stable support during times of distress, or they may have difficulty accepting support from their partner due to feelings of unworthiness or fear of dependency.

Need for patience and understanding

Navigating a relationship with someone who lives with disorganized attachment requires immense patience and understanding. The partner must recognize the unique emotional challenges their loved one faces and be willing to offer compassionate support.

Impact on relationship satisfaction

The challenges of disorganized attachment can have a significant impact on overall relationship satisfaction and stability. Frequent conflict, emotional distance, and uncertainty can contribute to decreased relationship satisfaction.

Seeking External Support

Couples may find it beneficial to seek outside support, such as couples therapy or counseling, to help them navigate the complexities of disorganized attachment. Professional counseling can provide insights and strategies for fostering healthier and more supportive relationship dynamics.

Address the misconceptions

Misconception: Disorganized people are simply emotionally unstable or unpredictable.

Reality: Disorganized attachment is a complex response to early trauma and inconsistent caregiving. It is not simply a matter of emotional instability, but rather a coping mechanism formed in response to adverse experiences.

Misconception: Disorganized attachment is impossible to change.

Reality: While disorganized attachment may present unique challenges, with therapeutic support and a safe and nurturing environment, individuals can work to develop more secure and organized attachment patterns.

Misconception: Disorganized attachment is always the result of severe abuse.

Reality: Disorganized attachment can be associated with severe abuse or neglect, but it can also develop in response to other adverse experiences that create conflicting emotional responses in the individual.

Misconception: Fearful avoidant attachment and disorganized attachment are the same thing.

Reality: Fearful avoidant attachment and disorganized attachment are distinct attachment styles with different characteristics and underlying dynamics. While both attachment styles can be influenced by early adverse experiences, they manifest differently in relationships. While the basic mechanism that differentiates fearful avoidant attachment from disorganized attachment is fear, the way that fear manifests and influences their coping behaviors is what distinguishes them.

In summary, disorganized attachment is a fascinating and complex attachment style characterized by a bewildering mix of conflicting behaviors and emotional responses. It deviates from the more defined secure, avoidant, and anxious attachment styles, making it both challenging and fascinating to understand. Individuals with disorganized attachment often experience uncertainty when seeking support or protection, leading to confusing and sometimes anxious behaviors in relationships.

As we continue our exploration of attachment styles, the next chapter will further explore the subtypes that emerge from the major insecure attachments. By examining these nuances, we aim to gain a more complete understanding of the complexities of human attachment.

Chapter 7: Insecure Attachment Subtypes: Understanding the Different Ways We Bond

Attachment theory offers valuable insights into how individuals form and maintain relationships, influencing their emotional well-being and interpersonal dynamics. While the major attachment styles (secure, anxious, avoidant, and disorganized) provide a broad framework for understanding relationship patterns, the complexity of human experience warrants closer examination. This is where attachment subtypes come into play, providing a more nuanced understanding of individuals' attachment behaviors and emotional responses.

Importance of subtypes

Attachment subtypes allow us to delve deeper into the various dimensions of attachment styles, recognizing that each individual is unique and may exhibit a mix of behaviors associated with different styles. Subtypes offer a more accurate representation of how attachment patterns manifest in real-life relationships and interactions. They help us appreciate the complexity of human emotions and experiences, and how past trauma or caregiving experiences shape attachment behaviors.

Navigating nuances

As we explore attachment subtypes, it is essential to recognize that categorizing individuals into a single style is an oversimplification. Humans are multifaceted beings, and attachment styles exist on a spectrum rather than in rigid boxes. People may exhibit different tendencies and responses based on different situations and relationship contexts.

The attachment subtypes:

1. **Anxious/Preoccupied Attachment:**
   a. Anxious-Ambivalent: Individuals with this subtype tend to be overly dependent on their partners and may become excessively preoccupied with their relationships.
   b. Anxious-Avoidant: This subtype exhibits both anxious and avoidant behaviors, resulting in a push-pull dynamic in relationships. They desire intimacy but are also afraid of being hurt, leading to conflicting behaviors.

2. **Avoidant Attachment:**
   a. Fearful-Avoidant: Individuals with this subtype desire close relationships but are afraid of getting hurt. They may exhibit avoidant behaviors but also long for emotional connection.
   b. Dismissive-Avoidant: This subtype tends to avoid emotional intimacy and may have a dismissive attitude towards their own feelings and needs as well as their partner's.

3. **Disorganized Attachment:**
   a. Disoriented: This subtype displays erratic and confused behaviors in relationships due to unresolved traumas or inconsistent caregiving

experiences in childhood. They may experience fear and confusion when seeking comfort from their attachment figures.

a. Anxious Ambivalent Attachment

The anxious-ambivalent attachment style is a subtype of the original anxious attachment style and shares some similarities with the broader category. Both styles are characterized by a deep fear of rejection and abandonment, which leads individuals to crave intimacy and closeness in their relationships. They may experience overwhelming anxiety about their partner's availability and love, and seek reassurance and validation to alleviate their fears.

However, the main difference between the anxious-ambivalent subtype and the original anxious attachment style is the intensity of their behaviors and emotional responses. Anxious-ambivalent individuals tend to display more extreme and intense behaviors than individuals with the general anxious attachment style.

In the general anxious attachment style, individuals may display some clingy and demanding behaviors, seeking reassurance from their partners and expressing fears of abandonment. They may be preoccupied with their relationships, but their behaviors may not be as extreme as those in the anxious-ambivalent subtype.

Anxious-ambivalent individuals, on the other hand, exhibit heightened emotional dependency and a greater need for constant closeness and reassurance. They may become overly preoccupied with their partners and engage in catastrophic thinking, imagining the worst-case scenarios in their relationships. Their fear of rejection and abandonment is more intense, leading to a higher level of emotional ups and downs.

Anxious-ambivalent attachment is typically formed in early childhood as a result of inconsistent or unpredictable caregiving. Children with this attachment style may have experienced caregivers who were sometimes responsive and affectionate, but at other times emotionally unavailable or dismissive of the child's needs. This inconsistency leaves the child feeling anxious and uncertain about the caregiver's availability, leading to a strong desire for proximity and closeness as a way to alleviate their anxiety.

Individuals with anxious-ambivalent attachment often display clingy and demanding behaviors in their relationships. They may become overly preoccupied with their partners and fear any sign of distance or disinterest. They seek constant reassurance of their partner's love and commitment and may feel insecure even in secure relationships. Anxious-ambivalent individuals may also be hypersensitive to relationship cues, overanalyzing their partner's actions and words for signs of rejection or abandonment.

Example

Meet Emily. Throughout her childhood, Emily's parents were inconsistently emotionally available due to their busy work schedules and personal issues. At times they were loving and attentive, but at other times they were emotionally distant. As a result, Emily developed an anxious-ambivalent attachment style in which she constantly sought validation and reassurance from her partners. In her romantic relationships, Emily is preoccupied with her partner's feelings and fears any signs of emotional distance. She often asks direct questions such as, "Do you still love me?" or "Are you sure you want to be with me?" Her fear of rejection leads her to seek constant reassurance, but she may also push her partner away with her excessive neediness.

Address the misconceptions

Misconception: Anxious-ambivalent people are always clingy and dependent.

Reality: While anxious-ambivalent individuals may seek closeness and reassurance, this does not mean that they are overly dependent in all areas of their lives. Their attachment style may primarily influence their romantic relationships, and they may demonstrate independence in other areas.

Misconception: Anxious-ambivalent attachment is a sign of emotional weakness.

Reality: Anxious-ambivalent attachment is a natural response to early experiences of inconsistent caregiving. It is not a sign of weakness, but reflects a genuine need for emotional support and connection.

Misconception: Anxious-ambivalent individuals are unhappy in their relationships.

Reality: Anxious-ambivalent individuals are capable of experiencing joy and love in relationships. However, their fear of abandonment and rejection can lead to emotional ups and downs in their relationships.

Misconception: Anxious-ambivalent attachment is a fixed personality trait.

Reality: While attachment styles are established early in life, they can be influenced and changed through self-awareness, personal growth, and healthy relationships. With support and self-reflection, individuals with anxious-ambivalent attachment can develop more secure attachment patterns.

b. Anxious Avoidant Attachment

Anxious-avoidant attachment is a unique and complex subtype that combines elements of both anxious and avoidant attachment styles. Individuals with this attachment pattern experience a deep longing for emotional closeness and intimacy and seek a deep connection with their partners. However, they also harbor deep-seated fears of rejection and vulnerability, creating an internal conflict in their approach to relationships.

The basic mechanisms of anxious-avoidant attachment involve a delicate balancing act between the desire for emotional connection and the need for self-preservation. On the one hand, these individuals crave the love and security that a close relationship can provide. Like those with anxious attachment, they seek validation and intimacy from their partners to assuage their fears and insecurities.

On the other hand, due to past experiences of disappointment or hurt, individuals with anxious-avoidant attachment are apprehensive about fully trusting their partners. They fear potential rejection and emotional pain, which leads them to develop protective measures to avoid being hurt. To protect themselves from vulnerability, they may engage in distancing behaviors, emotional withdrawal, or even push their partners away when emotional intimacy becomes too overwhelming. These behaviors create a paradoxical dynamic in which they both desire and distance themselves from intimacy.

The key difference between anxious-avoidant attachment and anxious attachment is how they deal with their anxiety. While those with anxious attachment respond to their fears by actively seeking reassurance and closeness, anxious-avoidant individuals respond by using avoidant strategies to protect themselves. This creates a push-pull dynamic in their relationships, where they crave emotional intimacy but struggle to fully embrace it for fear of being hurt.

Example

Meet Taylor, who embodies the anxious-avoidant attachment style. Taylor craves emotional connection and intimacy with their partner. They desire reassurance of their partner's love and commitment and seek comfort when feeling anxious or overwhelmed. However, when their partner tries to get close emotionally, Taylor's fear of emotional hurt triggers a defensive response. They may withdraw, become emotionally distant, or even create arguments to create emotional distance. Their push-pull behavior leaves their partner feeling confused and unsure about the relationship's stability.

Addressing Misconceptions

Misconception: Anxious-avoidant people are emotionally unavailable and commitment-phobic.

Reality: It's important to understand that while anxious-avoidant individuals may struggle with emotional vulnerability and intimacy, this does not mean they are uninterested in commitment or emotional connection. Their behavior is driven by a unique internal conflict in which they deeply desire emotional closeness but fear the potential hurt that comes with it. This conflict can lead to ambivalent behavior as they try to navigate between their desire for intimacy and their need to protect themselves.

Misconception: Anxious-avoidant attachment is a stable personality trait that cannot change.

Reality: While attachment styles, including anxious-avoidant, can be influenced by early experiences, it is essential to recognize that they are not fixed traits. With self-awareness, introspection, and therapeutic support, individuals with an anxious-avoidant attachment style can experience personal growth and transformation. By exploring their emotional needs and understanding the root causes of their attachment style, they can work to develop more secure attachment patterns and form healthier, more fulfilling relationships. It is a journey of self-discovery and healing that can lead to a more secure and satisfying emotional life.

Misconception: Anxious-avoidant people simply play "hard to get" or use mind games in relationships.

Reality: The anxious-avoidant attachment style is not a conscious game or strategy. It is a complex emotional response shaped by early life experiences and a genuine fear of vulnerability. Their push-pull behavior is a reflection of their internal struggle, torn between the desire for closeness and the fear of potential emotional hurt. It is important to approach individuals with an anxious-avoidant attachment style with empathy and understanding, recognizing that their emotional challenges are deeply rooted and require compassion rather than judgment. Building trust and creating a safe emotional environment can help them navigate their attachment style and form more secure relationships with their partners.

a. Fearful Avoidant Attachment

Fearful-avoidant attachment is a unique and complex subtype that blends elements of both anxious and avoidant attachment styles. Individuals with this attachment pattern experience a deep longing for emotional closeness and intimacy and seek a deep connection with their partners. However, they also harbor deep-seated fears of rejection and vulnerability that create an internal conflict in their approach to relationships.

The basic mechanisms of fearful-avoidant attachment involve a delicate balancing act between the desire for emotional connection and the need for self-preservation. On the one hand, these individuals crave the love and security that a close relationship can provide. Like those with anxious attachment, they seek validation and intimacy from their partners to assuage their fears and insecurities.

On the other hand, due to past experiences of disappointment or hurt, individuals with fearful-avoidant attachment are apprehensive about fully trusting their partners. They fear potential rejection and emotional pain, which leads them to develop defenses to avoid being hurt. To protect themselves from vulnerability, they may engage in distancing behaviors, emotional withdrawal, or even push their partners away when emotional intimacy becomes too overwhelming. These behaviors create a paradoxical dynamic in which they both desire and distance themselves from intimacy.

The key difference between fearful-avoidant attachment and anxious attachment is how they deal with their fears. While those with anxious attachment respond to their fears by actively seeking reassurance and closeness, fearful-avoidant individuals respond with a mix of anxious and avoidant strategies to protect themselves. This creates a push-pull dynamic in their relationships, where they crave emotional intimacy but struggle to fully embrace it for fear of being hurt.

In addition, fearful-avoidant attachment differs from original avoidant attachment in the degree of anxiety and internal conflict they experience. Those with avoidant attachment typically suppress their emotions and distance themselves from emotional intimacy, believing they can handle their feelings independently. However, fearful-avoidant people experience greater levels of internal turmoil and anxiety, oscillating between a desire for emotional connection and a fear of potential rejection.

In summary, fearful-avoidant attachment is a nuanced blend of anxious and avoidant attachment styles. Individuals with this pattern struggle with conflicting desires for emotional closeness and protection from potential rejection. The result is a complex interplay of behaviors that can make forming and maintaining relationships challenging for those with this attachment style. Understanding these distinct mechanisms can provide valuable insights into the complexities of human attachment and pave the way for more empathetic and supportive relationships.

Example

Meet David: David has a fearful avoidant attachment style that stems from early childhood experiences of inconsistent care and emotional neglect. As an adult, David deeply desires emotional intimacy and connection in relationships, but is plagued by an overwhelming fear of rejection and vulnerability. They struggle to trust others and are often torn between their desire for closeness and their need to protect themselves from potential emotional pain. In their romantic relationships, David may appear distant and emotionally unavailable, pushing their partner away when they feel emotionally overwhelmed. However, when their partner withdraws or becomes distant, David feels a surge of anxiety and attempts to pull them back in. This push-pull dynamic creates confusion and turmoil in their relationships, making it difficult for them to find a sense of emotional security.

Addressing Misconceptions

Misconception: Anxious-avoidant and fearful-avoidant attachment styles are the same.

Reality: Although both fearful-avoidant and anxious-avoidant attachment styles share some characteristics, there is one key feature that distinguishes them: the intensity of anxiety and emotional conflict. Fearful-avoidant individuals experience a deeper level of anxiety and inner turmoil than anxious-avoidant individuals. This can be overwhelming and confusing for fearful-avoidant individuals, who may feel caught between wanting closeness and intimacy and wanting to avoid it. On the other hand, anxious-avoidant individuals may have similar fears and internal conflicts, but the intensity may not be as severe as that of anxious-avoidant people.

Misconception: Fearful-avoidant people are just emotionally unstable or overly dramatic.

Reality: Fearful-avoidant attachment is not a result of being emotionally unstable or dramatic. It is a valid and natural response to early experiences that shaped their attachment style. Fearful-avoidant individuals may experience intense inner conflict and struggle with trusting others due to past trauma or inconsistent caregiving. Their emotional struggles are real and should not be dismissed as mere drama.

Misconception: Fearful-avoidant attachments cannot change, and these individuals are destined to have problematic relationships.

Reality: While fearful-avoidant attachment is deeply ingrained and can be challenging to navigate, it is not a fixed personality trait. Like all attachment styles, fearful-avoidant attachment can be influenced by later experiences, self-awareness, and therapeutic support. With patience, understanding, and a willingness to explore their fears and traumas, individuals with fearful-avoidant attachment can develop more secure attachment patterns and foster healthier relationships.

Misconception: Fearful-Avoidant individuals are distant and aloof by choice.

Reality: The emotional distance of fearful-avoidant individuals is not a conscious choice, but a coping mechanism developed from past experiences. They may have learned to suppress their feelings and needs to protect themselves from disappointment or rejection. Understanding the root of their emotional distance can help create a more empathetic and supportive environment for them to express their feelings and needs.

b. Dismissive Avoidant Attachment

Dismissive-avoidant attachment is a unique subtype that is distinct from the basic avoidant attachment style and the fearful-avoidant style. While all avoidant attachment styles share some common characteristics, dismissive-avoidant individuals have specific behaviors and attitudes that distinguish them from other attachment patterns.

Dismissive-avoidant individuals may still value their independence and self-reliance, much like those with basic avoidant attachment. However, dismissive-avoidant individuals tend to be more self-contained and less inclined to seek emotional support or intimacy from others. They downplay the importance of emotional closeness and may even view it as unnecessary or burdensome. Unlike basic avoidant individuals, who may feel uncomfortable with emotional intimacy but still desire it deep down, dismissive-avoidant individuals truly value their independence and may actively avoid emotional attachments altogether.

Differences from fearful-avoidant attachment:

Fearful-avoidant individuals experience intense inner turmoil and conflicting desires for emotional intimacy and distance. Dismissive-Avoidant individuals, on the other hand, do not experience the same level of internal conflict. They are more resolved in their preference for autonomy and may be less afraid of emotional intimacy. While both styles can lead to avoidance of emotional vulnerability, the underlying motivations and mechanisms are different.

The mechanisms underlying dismissive-avoidant attachment are rooted in past experiences, often with caregivers who were emotionally distant or unavailable. As children, dismissive-avoidant individuals may have learned to cope with their emotional needs by suppressing or denying their feelings. They may have received messages from their caregivers that emotions are a sign of weakness or that they should deal with their problems independently.

This early environment shaped their belief that dependence on others is unnecessary or unreliable, leading them to develop a strong sense of self-sufficiency. Over time, they have become adept at avoiding emotional vulnerability and keeping their emotions private. Rather than seeking support from others when faced with emotional challenges, they tend to withdraw and deal with their feelings internally.

Dismissive-avoidant individuals may appear emotionally distant or aloof in relationships. They may downplay the significance of emotional events or avoid discussing personal feelings. When faced with emotional situations, they may respond with rationality and logical thinking, dismissing the emotional aspect. Their strong focus on independence and self-sufficiency may make it difficult for them to rely on others or to show vulnerability.

In relationships, Dismissive-Avoidant individuals may appear distant and uninterested in emotional intimacy. They may prioritize personal space and independence, making it difficult for their partners to get emotionally close. While they may be able to form relationships, their reluctance to open up emotionally can create barriers to deep emotional connection.

Example

Meet Ryan: Ryan embodies a dismissive avoidant attachment style rooted in a childhood in which emotional needs were often ignored or dismissed by caregivers. As an adult, Ryan values independence and self-reliance and views emotional vulnerability as a sign of weakness. In romantic relationships, they may downplay their emotions and avoid discussing feelings or problems. They prefer to handle emotional challenges alone and may even withdraw or become emotionally distant when their partner seeks emotional closeness. This emotional detachment can create a sense of emotional distance in the relationship, leaving their partner feeling unimportant or neglected. Despite their desire for autonomy, Ryans may struggle with deep-seated feelings of loneliness and insecurity that they find difficult to acknowledge or express.

Addressing Misconceptions

Misconception: Dismissive-avoidant people are emotionless and cold-hearted.

Reality: Dismissive-avoidant attachment is not a lack of emotion or a cold-hearted demeanor. It is a learned coping mechanism developed from past experiences in which individuals have learned to minimize or dismiss their emotions as a way of protecting themselves from vulnerability. While they may appear emotionally detached, they are still experiencing emotions, but they have become adept at suppressing or minimizing their expression.

Misconception: Dismissive-Avoidant individuals are independent and don't need anyone.

Reality: Dismissive-Avoidant individuals may value independence and self-reliance, but that doesn't mean they don't want connection and support. They have learned to manage their emotions alone to protect themselves, but they still value relationships and can benefit from supportive and understanding partners who respect their need for personal space.

Misconception: Dismissive-avoidant attachment is a fixed personality trait that cannot change.

Reality: Like all attachment styles, dismissive-avoidant attachment can be influenced by later experiences and personal growth. While it may be deeply ingrained, with self-awareness and a willingness to explore their feelings and past experiences, individuals with dismissive-avoidant attachment can develop more secure attachment patterns and cultivate healthier relationships.

Misconception: Dismissive-avoidant individuals don't experience emotional pain.

Reality: Dismissive-avoidant individuals may be skilled at masking their emotions, but that doesn't mean they don't experience emotional pain. They may internalize their feelings and deal with them privately rather than seeking support from others. Their emotional pain is real, even if it is not readily apparent to those around them.

a. Disoriented Attachment

Disoriented attachment, also known as unresolved attachment, is a subtype that is distinct from the basic disorganized attachment style. While the disorganized attachment style shares elements of confusion and inconsistent behavior, disoriented attachment involves unresolved trauma or experiences with caregivers that lead to erratic and confused behavior in relationships.

Differences from Basic Disorganized Attachment

Basic disorganized attachment is characterized by a lack of organized strategies for interacting with caregivers. Children with basic disorganized attachment may exhibit behaviors such as freezing, appearing dazed, or exhibiting contradictory actions in the presence of their caregivers. In contrast, disoriented attachment involves unresolved trauma or unresolved experiences that cause a deeper level of confusion and disorganization in their approach to relationships. These unresolved issues can lead to more complex and chaotic behaviors, making it difficult for individuals with disoriented attachment to form stable and secure relationships.

The mechanisms underlying disoriented attachment are rooted in early childhood experiences of trauma or unresolved issues with caregivers. These experiences may include abusive or neglectful caregivers, witnessing violence, or other traumatic events that have not been adequately addressed or processed. These unresolved traumas create a sense of fear, confusion, and disorganization in the child's mind, making it difficult for them to develop a coherent attachment strategy.

As a result, individuals with disoriented attachment may exhibit erratic behavior in their relationships, alternating between seeking closeness and pushing others away. They may have difficulty trusting others or forming secure emotional attachments. Their unresolved traumas may also lead to emotional dysregulation and difficulty managing their emotions, which may further contribute to the disorganized and chaotic nature of their attachment style.

People with disoriented attachment may have difficulty understanding and expressing their emotions appropriately. They may have difficulty identifying their needs and may vacillate between seeking comfort from their caregivers and withdrawing from them. This internal conflict can lead to confusion and unpredictability in their relationships, making it difficult for them to form stable and secure connections with others.

Example

Meet Julia: Julia has a disoriented attachment style resulting from unresolved trauma and unpredictable caregiving in her childhood. As an adult, Julia experiences erratic and confused behavior in her relationships. She may seek emotional closeness and comfort from her partner, but at the same time feel overwhelmed and frightened by this intimacy. When faced with emotional distress or conflict, Julia may respond with contradictory behaviors, sometimes clinging to her partner for reassurance and sometimes pushing her away to protect herself from potential hurt. This inconsistency creates confusion and unpredictability in her relationships, making it difficult for her and her partner to establish a stable and secure emotional connection. Julia's unresolved traumas continue to impact her relationships as she deals with conflicting emotions and struggles to find a sense of safety and trust with her caregivers.

Addressing Misconceptions

Misconception: Disoriented attachment is a rare and unusual attachment style.

Reality: Disoriented attachment is a valid and relatively common attachment style, with a significant number of individuals exhibiting this attachment pattern. It may not be as widely recognized as secure, anxious, or avoidant attachment, but it plays a crucial role in understanding the complexities of human attachment and its impact on relationships.

Misconception: Disoriented attachment is the same as basic disorganized attachment.

Reality: While both disoriented attachment and basic disorganized attachment share elements of confusion and inconsistent behavior, disoriented attachment specifically involves unresolved trauma or experiences with caregivers. It represents a unique subset of disorganized attachment in which the individual's erratic behaviors stem from unresolved emotional issues rather than a generalized disorganization in attachment strategies.

Misconception: Disoriented attachment is a fixed and unchangeable trait.

Reality: Like other attachment styles, disoriented attachment can be influenced by early experiences, but it is not a fixed or unchangeable trait. With self-awareness, introspection, and therapeutic support, individuals with disoriented attachment can work to resolve unresolved traumas and experiences, leading to more secure attachment patterns and healthier relationships.

Misconception: Disoriented attachment is caused solely by early childhood experiences.

Reality: While early childhood experiences play an important role in the development of disoriented attachment, it can also be influenced by later life events and relationships. Traumatic experiences or significant losses in adulthood can contribute to disoriented attachment patterns, highlighting the ongoing impact of attachment dynamics throughout life.

Misconception: Disoriented attachment is always associated with severe trauma or abuse.

Reality: While disoriented attachment can be associated with traumatic experiences, it is not exclusively associated with severe abuse or trauma. It can result from a range of experiences, including inconsistent caregiving, neglect, or other stressful events. The impact of disorganized attachment can vary depending on an individual's resilience and coping mechanisms.

Misconception: Disoriented attachment is the same as fearful attachment.

Reality: Disoriented attachment and fearful attachment are different attachment styles. Fearful attachment involves a fear of both intimacy and rejection, resulting in a push-pull dynamic in relationships. On the other hand, disoriented attachment arises from unresolved trauma or experiences with caregivers, resulting in erratic and confused behavior when seeking support or comfort. While both styles can experience internal conflict, the underlying mechanisms and triggers for this conflict are very different.

Misconception: Disoriented attachment is a sign of emotional instability or mental illness.

Reality: Disorganized attachment is not itself a sign of emotional instability or mental illness. It is a pattern of attachment that results from unresolved emotional issues and trauma. Individuals with disoriented attachment can have fulfilling and healthy relationships with appropriate support, understanding, and self-awareness. Mental health issues, if present, should be addressed separately from attachment patterns.

In closing, attachment subtypes recognize the complexity of human emotions and experiences and emphasize that each person is unique and may exhibit a mix of behaviors associated with different styles. As we explore the anxious, avoidant, and disorganized attachment subtypes, it is important to avoid oversimplification and understand that attachment styles exist on a spectrum and can be influenced by different situations and relationship contexts.

In the next chapter, I will help you use a self-assessment to identify your attachment style and gain a deeper understanding of your tendencies in forming relationships with others. This self-awareness can lead to personal growth, the development of more secure attachment patterns, and the formation of healthier, more fulfilling relationships. By embracing the complexity of attachment, we can foster empathy and compassion and support ourselves and others in navigating the intricacies of human connection.

Chapter 8: What's Your Attachment Style?

Have you ever wondered about your attachment style?

Welcome to the Attachment and Emotional Expression Assessment! This simple and insightful assessment is designed to help you gain a better understanding of how you approach relationships, express your emotions, and cope with various situations involving your close relationships.

In this questionnaire, you will find a series of scenarios related to common relationship experiences. For each scenario, choose the answer that best represents your typical thoughts, feelings, and behaviors. Please answer each question honestly and instinctively, without overthinking your answers. Your genuine answers will provide the most accurate results.

The test has four options for each question: (a) Perfectly fine, I trust they'll be back. (b) I'm worried, I keep wondering when they'll be back. (c) I feel anxious, but I try not to show it. (d) I'm not sure, my feelings are mixed. Each response option corresponds to a specific score that is used to assess your attachment style and emotional expression tendencies.

After you complete the quiz, you will receive an interpretation of your results, indicating which attachment style may best describe your approach to relationships. The possible attachment styles are Secure, Anxious, Avoidant, and Disorganized.

Remember, there are no right or wrong answers in this assessment; it's about gaining insight into your unique emotional responses and coping mechanisms. Understanding these aspects of yourself can empower you to foster healthier, more fulfilling relationships and improve your emotional well-being.

Let's get started! For each scenario, choose the answer that resonates most with you, and we'll uncover fascinating insights about your attachment and emotional expression tendencies.

How do you usually feel when someone you care about is away for a long time?

a) Completely fine, I trust they'll be back.

b) Worried, I keep thinking about when they'll be back.

c) I feel anxious, but I try not to show it.

d) I'm not sure, my feelings are mixed.

When you have a fight with someone close to you, how do you usually react?

a) I try to discuss and resolve the issue calmly.

b) I feel very upset and seek reassurance from them.

c) I withdraw and need time alone to process my feelings.

d) I become unsure of how to react, and it varies.

How comfortable are you with opening up to others about your feelings and emotions?

a) Very comfortable, I have no problem expressing myself.

b) I find it difficult, but I try to share my feelings.

c) I'm selective about who I open up to, and it takes time.

d) I have difficulty expressing my feelings to others.

When you need support or comfort, what do you usually do?

a) Seek comfort from someone I trust.

b) Worry that I'll be a burden to others if I ask for help.

c) I prefer to deal with my feelings on my own.

d) I'm not sure how I usually deal with it.

How do you react when your partner or a close friend wants to spend time with you?

a) I'm always happy to spend time with them.

b) I feel a little overwhelmed, but usually agree.

c) I may feel stifled and need some space.

d) I'm not sure how I usually react.

When someone ends a relationship with you, how do you usually react?

a) Although it's upsetting, I understand that relationships can end.

b) I feel devastated and have a hard time letting go.

c) I may feel hurt, but I try to move on quickly.

d) I have mixed feelings about it.

How do you deal with conflict in your relationships?

a) I address them directly and try to find a solution.

b) I often worry that conflict will lead to abandonment.

c) I may avoid confrontation and hope the problem will go away.

d) I'm not sure how I usually deal with conflict.

In new relationships, how quickly do you tend to trust the other person?

a) I trust people until they give me a reason not to.

b) It takes me a while to build trust in new relationships.

c) I may trust at first, but then become cautious.

d) I'm not sure how to approach trust in new relationships.

How often do you seek affirmation or approval from others?

a) I don't seek validation; I have confidence in myself.

b) I sometimes seek validation, especially during difficult times.

c) I often seek validation and reassurance from others.

d) I don't know how often I seek validation.

How do you feel about relying on others for emotional support?

a) I'm comfortable relying on others for support.

b) I'm afraid I'll be a burden to others if I rely on them.

c) I prefer to manage my emotions independently.

d) I'm not sure how I feel about depending on others.

How do you usually deal with feelings of jealousy in a relationship?

a) I communicate my feelings openly and work through them.

b) I feel extremely jealous and need constant reassurance.

c) I may become distant or avoid confronting the issue.

d) I'm not sure how I usually deal with jealousy.

When someone you care about is going through a difficult time, how do you respond?

a) I offer my support and try to help them through it.

b) I worry constantly about their well-being.

c) I may feel overwhelmed and not know how to help.

d) I'm not sure how I usually respond to their difficult times.

How do you handle rejection or criticism?

a) I take it in stride and use it as an opportunity to learn.

b) I feel devastated and question my worth.

c) I may become defensive or avoid situations where I might be rejected.

d) I'm not sure how I usually deal with rejection.

What do you think about emotional intimacy in relationships?

a) I value emotional intimacy and actively seek it out.

b) I desire emotional intimacy, but it also makes me anxious.

c) I prefer to keep my feelings to myself most of the time.

d) I'm not sure how I feel about emotional intimacy.

How do you usually react to changes or disturbances in your relationships?

a) I adapt well and try to find solutions to the changes.

b) I become anxious and worry about the stability of the relationship.

c) I may withdraw and need time to process the changes.

d) I'm not sure how I usually react to relationship changes.

Scores and their interpretation

Score Range: 51 - 64

Interpretation: Secure Attachment Style

A high score in this range indicates that the individual has a secure attachment style. They are comfortable with emotional intimacy, openly express their feelings, and seek support when needed. They are generally confident in themselves and have healthy ways of dealing with conflict and relationship change.

Score range: 36 - 50

Interpretation: Anxious Attachment Style

A score in this range indicates an anxious attachment style. Individuals with this style tend to worry about the stability of their relationships, frequently seek reassurance, and may have difficulty expressing their emotions openly. They may also have difficulty coping with rejection and criticism.

Score range: 21 - 35

Interpretation: Avoidant Attachment Style

Scores in this range indicate an avoidant attachment style. People with this style may have difficulty with emotional intimacy and may prefer to keep their emotions to themselves. They may also withdraw when faced with conflict or change in their relationships.

Score range: 6 - 20

Interpretation: Disorganized Attachment Style

A score in this range indicates a disorganized attachment style. Individuals with this style may have mixed and unpredictable reactions in relationships. They may have difficulty expressing their emotions, dealing with conflict, and trusting others. Disorganized attachment is characterized by a lack of a coherent pattern in approaching relationships, often resulting from early inconsistent caregiving experiences.

Score range: 5 or below

Interpretation: Inconclusive

A very low score may indicate that the participant did not respond consistently or honestly. This score may not be a clear representation of their attachment style and emotional tendencies.

This Attachment and Emotional Expression Assessment is for self-assessment purposes only. It is not a formal diagnosis or a substitute for professional counseling. While the quiz provides insights, human emotions are complex and the results may not capture the full picture. If you feel distressed or need support, consult a qualified mental health professional. Prioritize your well-being and remember that seeking professional help is a proactive step toward emotional growth and resilience.

Reflections on test results and emotional well-being

If you are feeling upset or anxious about your test results, please remember that this assessment is just one tool among many for understanding complex human emotions and behaviors. The results do not define you as a person, nor do they dictate the course of your relationships or emotional well-being. Here are some reassuring points to consider:

Normal variability

Human emotions and attachment styles are diverse and multifaceted. It's normal to experience a range of emotions and have different ways of relating to others. There is no "right" or "perfect" attachment style, and everyone's emotional journey is unique.

Room for growth

Regardless of your initial results, it's important to recognize that attachment styles and emotional expressions can be influenced by various factors, including past experiences, personal growth, and current circumstances. People can learn and develop healthier ways of relating and expressing emotions over time.

Opportunity for self-reflection

The assessment provides an opportunity for self-reflection and self-awareness. Becoming more aware of your emotional tendencies and attachment style can be the first step toward personal growth and positive change in your relationships.

Seek support

If the results of the assessment make you feel uncomfortable or uncertain, consider speaking with a mental health professional, such as a therapist or counselor. They can provide a safe space to explore your feelings, work through any challenges, and offer guidance on how to foster healthier relationships.

Embrace your journey

Remember that personal growth is an ongoing process, and we all have moments of growth and self-discovery throughout our lives. Be kind to yourself and embrace the journey to better understand and accept yourself.

Strengths and Resilience

Recognize your strengths and resilience in dealing with life's challenges. We all have the ability to adapt, learn, and develop healthier coping mechanisms.

Connections matter

Regardless of your attachment style, fostering meaningful connections and open communication in your relationships can lead to more satisfying and fulfilling interactions with others.

You are not alone

Many people experience moments of uncertainty or self-doubt. Remember that you are not alone in your journey, and reaching out for support is a sign of strength, not weakness.

Ultimately, this assessment is a starting point, and its results should be taken as a general assessment rather than a definitive conclusion. You have the power to shape your emotional well-being and cultivate the relationships you desire.

So take a deep breath, be gentle with yourself, and remember that you have the potential for growth and positive change. Embrace your unique emotional journey and remember that seeking support and guidance is a sign of strength. You have the capacity to make meaningful and fulfilling connections with others. Trust in your ability to learn and grow as you continue on your path to emotional well-being.

How did your questionnaire go?

Did you already know about your behavioral tendencies, or were you surprised by the results?

No matter what your results were, don't worry.

I still have a lot to tell you. In the next chapter, we will talk about the most common barriers that prevent us from changing.

Chapter 9: Overcoming Barriers to Change

Welcome to the crucial chapter, "Overcoming Barriers to Change. Now is the time to delve into the essentials of understanding and overcoming the challenges that can arise when trying to improve your attachment style. As you embark on this journey of personal growth, it is important to be prepared to face the obstacles that may impede your progress.

Change, while attainable and achievable, is rarely a smooth and effortless process. It requires introspection, determination, and resilience to navigate the maze of obstacles that lie ahead. It is time to shed light on the concept of barriers and illuminate the pathways to overcoming them effectively.

Imagine that you have identified aspects of your attachment style that you would like to transform, envisioning a more satisfying and healthy relationship with yourself and others. You set out with hope and enthusiasm, eager to make positive changes. Along the way, however, you encounter obstacles that seem to thwart your efforts.

These barriers to change can take many forms: some may be internal, woven into your beliefs and past experiences, while others may be external, such as societal norms, rigid family patterns, or the reactions of those around you. Recognizing and understanding these obstacles is the first step in overcoming them.

It is important to recognize, however, that barriers to successful and satisfying romantic relationships are not limited to any one attachment style. These barriers transcend attachment labels and can be experienced by people from all walks of life. Whether you find security in the arms of a partner, struggle with anxiety in relationships, or tend to keep emotional distance, common obstacles can arise that hinder the growth and longevity of the relationship.

Understanding and overcoming these common barriers is critical for anyone seeking to build a healthy and thriving romantic partnership. By shedding light on these universal challenges, we can gain valuable insights and tools to overcome them, fostering resilience and personal growth within ourselves and our relationships.

Throughout this chapter, we will explore these common threads that intertwine all types of attachment. From fear of vulnerability and past trauma to self-doubt and communication barriers, we will delve into the heart of these barriers and examine how they impact our romantic lives. In doing so, we hope to equip you with the knowledge and strategies you need to forge deeper connections, cultivate emotional intimacy, and transcend the limitations that may have held you back in the past.

Keep in mind that you are not alone in this endeavor. Countless others have made the same journey, and their stories of triumph over adversity serve as a beacon of inspiration. By learning from their experiences and applying the wisdom they have gained, you will be able to overcome the obstacles that come your way.

Common Obstacles that Prevent Strong Connections in Relationships

Fear of vulnerability and emotional intimacy

People with insecure attachment styles often find it difficult to open up emotionally and be vulnerable with others. Past experiences of rejection or emotional neglect may have instilled a fear of being hurt or abandoned, causing them to put up emotional walls and avoid deep connection. As a result, forming meaningful and intimate relationships becomes a daunting task.

- Practice emotional self-awareness: Cultivate a deeper understanding of your emotions and the reasons for your fear of vulnerability. Reflect on past experiences that may have contributed to this fear.

- Start Small: Gradually open up to your partner about less sensitive topics before diving into deeper emotions. Take it one step at a time and allow yourself to become more comfortable with vulnerability.

- Communicate your feelings: Share your concerns with your partner and express your desire to work through these fears together. Honest communication can foster trust and support.

Example: You find it challenging to express your deeper emotions and thoughts to your partner, fearing that they might judge or reject you.

Practical Strategies:

1. Start by sharing something light, like your favorite childhood memory, and gradually move towards more vulnerable topics as you feel more comfortable.

2. When you feel emotionally triggered, take a moment to identify the underlying emotion and communicate it to your partner, saying, "I'm

feeling a bit vulnerable right now, but I'd like to share something with you."

3. Take small steps: Gradually challenge your fear of vulnerability by sharing one more sensitive topic at a time. Celebrate each step you take in opening up emotionally.

Negative self-beliefs and low self-esteem

Deep-seated negative beliefs about themselves can plague those with insecure attachment styles. They may perceive themselves as unworthy of love and affection, believing that they are fundamentally flawed or undeserving of happiness. Such low self-esteem can sabotage attempts to improve their attachment style by undermining their confidence in their ability to change and grow.

- Challenge negative thoughts: Whenever negative self-beliefs arise, question their validity. Ask yourself for evidence that supports or contradicts these beliefs.

- Celebrate your achievements: Acknowledge your strengths and accomplishments, no matter how small they may seem. Practicing self-compassion can help counteract low self-esteem.

- Seek support: Consider therapy or counseling to address underlying issues that contribute to low self-esteem. A professional can provide guidance and tools to boost your self-esteem.

Example: You often feel inadequate in your relationship, believing that you're not good enough for your partner.

Practical strategies:

1. Use positive self-talk: Challenge negative thoughts with positive, realistic affirmations. For example, if you catch yourself thinking, "I'm not good enough," replace it with, "I have many valuable qualities that make me worthy of love.

2. Seek external validation: Talk to friends or loved ones who can provide an objective perspective on your strengths and accomplishments. Sometimes hearing positive feedback from others can help counteract self-doubt.

3. Explore your interests: Engage in activities and hobbies that you truly enjoy and excel at. Focusing on your passions can boost your self-esteem and remind you of your unique talents.

4. Practice gratitude: Each day, write down one thing you are grateful for. It could be a kind gesture you did for someone, a personal accomplishment, or a positive quality you possess.

5. Set achievable goals: Break down larger tasks into smaller, more manageable goals. Celebrate each step you take toward those goals and recognize your progress and efforts.

6. Limit social media comparison: Avoid comparing yourself to others on social media. Remember that people often present a curated version of their lives, and comparing yourself to unrealistic standards can undermine your self-esteem.

Resistance to change due to past experiences and trauma

Past trauma, such as betrayal or neglect, can create resistance to change. The familiar patterns of an insecure attachment style may provide a sense of comfort or protection, even if they are unhealthy. Stepping outside of these patterns can trigger fear and reluctance to confront the unknown, hindering personal growth.

- Practice mindfulness: Be present with your emotions and thoughts, and acknowledge how past experiences may be influencing your reactions in the present.

- Seek healing: Engage in therapeutic techniques such as Eye Movement Desensitization and Reprocessing (EMDR) or Trauma-Focused Cognitive Behavioral Therapy (TF-CBT) to address and heal past traumas.

Example: You're reluctant to give up control in the relationship because past experiences have taught you that vulnerability leads to pain.

Practical Strategies:

1. Educate yourself: Learn about attachment theory and how past experiences can shape your current attachment style. Understanding the origins of your resistance can make it easier to work through.

2. Create a safe environment: Establish a safe space in your relationship where you and your partner can communicate openly, free of judgment or blame.

3. Practice emotional regulation: Learn coping techniques, such as deep breathing or grounding exercises, to manage overwhelming emotions that may arise from past triggers.

4. Journaling: Write about your feelings and experiences to process emo-

tions related to past trauma. Journaling can provide clarity and insight for healing.

5. Practice self-compassion: Be kind to yourself during this process. Healing and growth take time, and it's important to treat yourself with understanding and patience.

Defensiveness and difficulty accepting feedback

Individuals with an insecure attachment style may become defensive when faced with feedback or constructive criticism. This defensiveness arises as a coping mechanism to protect themselves from feelings of inadequacy or vulnerability. Unfortunately, this defensiveness can block the potential for growth and hinder the receptivity to learn from their experiences.

- Practice active listening: When receiving feedback, focus on truly understanding your partner's perspective before formulating a response.

- Pause and reflect: Before reacting defensively, take a moment to process the feedback and consider whether there may be some truth to it.

- Use "I" statements: When expressing your thoughts, use "I" statements instead of blaming language. This approach promotes open communication and reduces defensiveness.

Example: When your partner offers constructive criticism, you feel attacked and immediately become defensive.

Practical Strategies:

1. Recognize defensiveness: The first step is to become aware of your defensive reactions. Look for physical cues such as tense muscles or racing thoughts that may indicate defensiveness.

2. Take a time-out: If you notice yourself becoming defensive during a conversation, take a short break. Step away from the situation, take a deep breath, and calm yourself before returning to the conversation.

3. Empathize with your partner: Put yourself in your partner's shoes and try to understand his or her perspective. Remind yourself that their intention is to improve the relationship, not to attack you personally.

4. Practice mindful communication: Focus on listening to your partner without interrupting or planning your response. Acknowledge their feelings and validate their experience.

5. Ask for clarification: If you're not sure about something your partner has said, ask them to elaborate or clarify their point. This shows that you are genuinely interested in understanding them better.

6. Respond Calmly: When it's time to respond, do so in a calm and collected manner. Avoid reacting impulsively or emotionally, as this can escalate the situation.

7. Seek solutions together: Instead of dwelling on the criticism itself, focus on finding solutions together. Discuss how you can work as a team to address the issues raised.

8. Practice self-compassion: Remind yourself that no one is perfect and that it's okay to have areas for growth. Treat yourself with kindness and understanding throughout the process.

9. Seek feedback gradually: If receiving feedback feels overwhelming, ask

your partner to start with smaller, less sensitive issues. Gradually build up to more significant issues as you become more comfortable with the process.

Fear of abandonment or rejection

The fear of abandonment or rejection looms large in the minds of those with insecure attachment styles. This fear can lead to clingy behavior or emotional withdrawal as they try to protect themselves from potential heartbreak. Ironically, these very behaviors can strain relationships and, in some cases, become a self-fulfilling prophecy.

- **Identify Pattern Behaviors**: Recognize behaviors driven by the fear of abandonment, such as pushing your partner away or becoming overly dependent.

- **Practice Self-Soothing**: Develop coping mechanisms to manage anxiety and fear. Engage in activities that bring you comfort and calmness.

Example: You avoid expressing your needs or desires to your partner because you're afraid they'll leave if they don't agree.

Practical Strategies:

1. Identify triggers: Identify situations or behaviors that trigger your fear of abandonment. Understanding your triggers can help you deal with them more effectively.

2. Communicate your feelings: Share your fears with your partner and express how you're working to overcome them. Open communication can foster understanding and support.

3. Challenge assumptions: Challenge the assumptions underlying your fear of rejection. Is there evidence to support your belief that your partner will leave if they don't agree with you? Challenging these assumptions can help you gain perspective.

4. Practice self-examination: Remind yourself that your feelings and needs are valid and deserve to be acknowledged. It's important to acknowledge and honor your feelings.

5. Set boundaries: Set clear boundaries in your relationship to ensure that your needs are respected. Setting healthy boundaries can reduce anxiety and promote a sense of safety.

6. Practice mindfulness: When feelings of anxiety arise, practice mindfulness techniques such as deep breathing or grounding exercises to stay present and manage anxiety.

7. Explore past experiences: Reflect on past experiences that may have contributed to your fear of abandonment. Understanding their impact can help you heal and grow.

8. Build a support network: Surround yourself with friends or family who provide a supportive and caring environment. A strong support network can provide reassurance during difficult times.

9. Focus on self-growth: Cultivate personal growth and self-actualization outside of your relationship. Engage in hobbies, interests, and personal goals that bring you joy and fulfillment.

Changing our attachment style and building healthier relationships is not easy.

In this chapter, we explored some of the barriers that can stop us from making progress.

These barriers include fear of vulnerability, negative self-beliefs, resistance due to past trauma, defensiveness, and fear of abandonment.

In the next chapter, we'll talk about how to build trust, get closer to your partner emotionally, and other important things for a strong relationship.

Chapter 10: Building Trust and Intimacy in Romantic Relationships

In a romantic relationship, trust and intimacy are like the building blocks that hold everything together. They create a safe space where partners can be themselves, share their deepest thoughts, and feel emotionally secure. Developing trust and intimacy becomes even more important when one or both partners have struggled with insecure attachment patterns in the past. Although it may seem challenging, it is entirely possible to build these vital components, even if there have been struggles along the way.

Trust is the foundation of any healthy relationship. It's about relying on each other, being dependable, and keeping promises. When trust is present, partners feel safe sharing their innermost feelings, knowing they won't be judged or betrayed. But for those who have faced insecure attachment issues, trust may be harder to establish. Past experiences of feeling abandoned or unimportant can cast a shadow over the present, making it difficult to fully trust a partner.

Intimacy, on the other hand, goes beyond physical affection. It's the emotional closeness and connection that allows partners to be truly intimate. This emotional bond strengthens the relationship and fosters a sense of belonging. For people who have struggled with insecure attachment, however, intimacy can be daunting. Fear of being vulnerable or getting hurt may cause them to keep their emotions in check.

Despite these challenges, building trust and intimacy is both worthwhile and achievable. It requires patience, understanding, and a willingness to work together. By taking practical steps and implementing strategies, partners can forge a deeper and more fulfilling connection. In this chapter, we will explore these actionable steps and offer guidance on how to create a safe and open environment for communication, establish reliability and consistency, and encourage emotional vulnerability.

We will also discuss the importance of resolving conflict constructively, since disagreements are natural in any relationship. Through mindful communication and empathy, partners can find common ground and grow stronger together. We'll discuss the importance of emotional intimacy and how being emotionally present for each other can lead to a more satisfying and harmonious partnership.

It is crucial to keep in mind that building trust and intimacy is a process that takes time and effort. Partners need to be compassionate with each other and understand that past experiences may influence their behaviors and reactions. The journey to deeper trust and intimacy may have its ups and downs, but with dedication and a shared commitment to growth, partners can overcome insecure attachment issues and create a more secure and loving bond.

In the following paragraphs, we will explore practical strategies for building trust and intimacy, offering guidance and insights to help partners navigate this transformative journey together. By taking these steps, couples can strengthen their connection, foster a deeper sense of emotional security, and experience the joy of a truly intimate and fulfilling romantic relationship.

Establishing Emotional Safety

In every thriving romantic relationship, emotional safety is of paramount importance. It provides a solid foundation for partners to express themselves and be vulnerable. Creating a safe and non-judgmental space requires a conscious effort to foster trust and acceptance between partners.

Create a Safe and Judgment-Free Space

To create emotional safety, it is essential to create an environment where both individuals feel safe to share their thoughts, feelings, and vulnerabilities. Encouraging open expression is fundamental to this process. Partners should feel free to communicate openly and honestly, knowing that their thoughts and feelings are valued and respected. This active encouragement of open communication helps build trust and deepens the emotional bond between them.

Empathy is another critical aspect of creating emotional safety. When one partner speaks, the other should be an empathetic listener, offering undivided attention. Empathy involves understanding and validating the other person's feelings and experiences, even if they are different from your own. Interrupting or dismissing their feelings can create barriers to open communication and cause them to withdraw emotionally.

Vulnerability is an essential component of emotional safety. Both partners should feel comfortable being vulnerable with each other, which requires courage and trust. Vulnerability involves revealing one's true self, including fears, insecurities, and dreams. Leading by example and showing vulnerability encourages the other partner to do the same, fostering deeper emotional intimacy and connection.

To maintain emotional safety, it is important to avoid criticism and blame during disagreements or conflicts. Instead of pointing fingers, partners should strive to understand each other's perspectives and feelings. Conflict can become an opportunity for growth and understanding, rather than an opportunity to assign blame. Adopting a non-judgmental attitude is crucial to maintaining emotional safety and ensuring that both partners feel respected and valued.

In addition, practicing non-defensiveness is critical to maintaining emotional safety. When one partner expresses concern or emotion, the other should avoid becoming defensive. Defensiveness can hinder communication and create barriers that make it difficult to address underlying issues. Instead, partners should strive to understand each other's feelings and experiences, validate their feelings, and reassure them that they are heard and valued.

Avoid Blame and Defensiveness during Disagreements

In times of disagreement, it is important to avoid blame and defensiveness to maintain emotional safety. Using "I" statements instead of "you" statements helps to express feelings and needs without pointing fingers. This promotes constructive communication and a willingness to listen without feeling attacked.

Seeking understanding is key in disagreements. Partners should take the time to understand each other's point of view without becoming defensive or trying to prove their own point of view. Instead, they can ask open-ended questions to gain insight into their partner's feelings and thoughts, demonstrating that they value the other person's perspective and are willing to work together toward a solution.

Taking breaks when necessary can also contribute to emotional safety during conflict. Emotions can run high during disagreements, making it difficult to have a productive conversation. Agreeing to take a break and revisit the topic when both partners are calmer allows for a more constructive discussion, free of blame and defensiveness.

Focusing on finding solutions and compromises that meet the needs of both partners helps maintain emotional safety. Rather than dwelling on past mistakes or assigning blame, partners should work together as a team, seeking common ground and fostering a sense of partnership in the relationship.

Acknowledging and repairing mistakes made during disagreements is essential to emotional safety. Taking responsibility for one's actions and offering a sincere apology when necessary shows respect for the other partner's feelings and helps repair any emotional damage caused. Demonstrating a commitment to emotional safety and maintaining a healthy relationship strengthens the bond between partners.

Creating a safe and non-judgmental space where partners can express themselves openly and work through disagreements with empathy and understanding fosters emotional safety. This strong foundation paves the way for deeper trust and intimacy in the relationship, fostering a more connected and fulfilling bond between partners. Building emotional safety is an ongoing process that requires active efforts by both partners to maintain open communication, empathy, and mutual respect.

Communicate Openly and Honestly

Effective and open communication is a fundamental aspect of building trust in a romantic relationship. When partners communicate openly and honestly, it fosters an environment of authenticity and emotional safety. This creates a space where both individuals can express themselves freely and honestly without fear of judgment or criticism.

To cultivate open communication, it's vital to be transparent and authentic with one another. This means sharing thoughts and feelings honestly and avoiding hidden agendas or passive-aggressive behavior. By being open about our feelings and thoughts, we create a sense of trust and allow our partners to see our true selves.

Partner A: "I've been feeling a little overwhelmed lately with work and personal issues. I just wanted to let you know because I might need some extra support and understanding.

Partner B: "Thank you for sharing this with me. I'm here for you and you can always count on me for support. Is there anything in particular you'd like me to do to help you through this?"

In addition to openness, it is important to actively listen when our partner is speaking. Active listening means giving them our full attention, refraining from interrupting, and showing genuine interest in their perspective. Validating their feelings, even if we may not fully agree, helps create a deeper emotional connection.

Partner A: "I had a difficult conversation with my boss today, and it left me feeling frustrated and upset.

Partner B: "I'm sorry to hear that you had a difficult time. It's essential to me that you feel comfortable talking about it. Please know that I'm here to listen if you need to talk.

To ensure constructive communication, it is beneficial to use "I" statements. This approach allows us to express our feelings and needs without blaming or accusing our partner. For example, we might say, "I feel hurt when..." instead of using accusatory language like, "You always do that..."

Partner A: "I feel hurt when plans change last minute without discussing it with me. It makes me feel like my opinions don't matter."

Partner B: "I understand, and I'm sorry for not considering your feelings. I realize how important it is to involve you in decisions that affect us both. Let's find a way to communicate better and make decisions together."

Respect is another key element of open communication. It is important to respect each other's boundaries, opinions, and individuality. By respecting our partner's perspective and choices, we foster a sense of safety and trust in the relationship.

Partner A: "I'm thinking about taking on a new project at work, but I wanted to discuss it with you first."

Partner B: "I appreciate that you value my input. Let's talk about the project, and I'll support you no matter what you decide."

We must also avoid assuming what our partner is thinking or feeling, as mind-reading can lead to misunderstandings and miscommunication. Instead, asking open-ended questions and seeking clarification helps us gain insight into their feelings and perspectives.

Partner A: "You seem distant lately. Is there something on your mind?"

Partner B: "I've been feeling a bit stressed about work, but I didn't want to burden you with it."

Partner A: "I want you to feel comfortable sharing your worries with me. We're a team, and I'm here to support you through the ups and downs."

Addressing past issues is essential to building trust through communication. If there have been breaches of trust or communication breakdowns in the past, it's important to address them openly and honestly. Acknowledging the impact of these issues and working together to find solutions and healing is essential to the growth of the relationship.

Partner A: "I want to talk about what happened last week when we had that argument. I felt hurt by some of the things you said."

Partner B: "I'm sorry for my part in the argument. I didn't mean to hurt you, and I'm willing to work on my communication to avoid such situations in the future."

Empathy plays an important role in fostering open communication. Putting ourselves in our partner's shoes and trying to understand their feelings and point of view helps build emotional connection and a deeper sense of trust.

Partner A: "I'm nervous about the job interview tomorrow. I really want to get this job."

Partner B: "I understand how important this is for you. You've prepared well, and I have confidence in your abilities. Remember, I'll be rooting for you and supporting you no matter what."

Building trust through open communication is a gradual process that requires patience. It's important to be patient with each other's communication styles and to recognize that growth and progress take time.

If challenges persist or past traumas affect the relationship, it may be beneficial to seek the guidance of a couples therapist. A trained professional can help facilitate constructive communication and provide valuable insights for building trust.

In conclusion, open and honest communication is the foundation of trust in a romantic relationship. By being transparent, respectful, and empathetic, partners can create a strong bond of trust that fosters a more intimate and fulfilling connection.

Building Trust

In any love relationship, trust is the cornerstone that cements the bond between partners. Building and maintaining trust requires consistent effort and genuine honesty.

Be Reliable and Consistent

One of the most important ways to build trust is to be reliable and consistent. When you make commitments and promises to your partner, keep them. For example, if you agree to do certain household chores, make sure you do them as promised. This reliability shows your partner that he or she can count on you to keep your word and that you are dependable.

Consistency in both actions and words is crucial to building trust. For example, if you express love and affection to your partner, make sure your actions reflect those feelings. Consistency helps reassure your partner that your words are genuine, leading to a stronger sense of trust in the relationship.

Reliability goes beyond fulfilling obligations; it also includes being emotionally available and supportive. For example, if your partner is facing a difficult situation at work or in his or her personal life, be there to listen and offer support. Being consistently present in both good times and challenging moments helps create a sense of security and reassurance that fosters trust.

Avoid Deception

Trust cannot thrive in an environment of deception. Honesty is the foundation of trust in any relationship. Be honest with your partner and avoid withholding important information. For example, if you made a mistake or forgot to tell your partner something important, be upfront about it. Hiding information can lead to a breach of trust, while honest communication strengthens it.

Partner A: "I want to talk about what happened last week when we had that argument. I felt hurt by some of the things you said."

Partner B: "I'm sorry for my part in the argument. I didn't mean to hurt you, and I'm willing to work on my communication to avoid such situations in the future."

Empathy plays an important role in fostering open communication. Putting ourselves in our partner's shoes and trying to understand their feelings and point of view helps build emotional connection and a deeper sense of trust.

Partner A: "I'm nervous about the job interview tomorrow. I really want to get this job."

Partner B: "I understand how important this is for you. You've prepared well, and I have confidence in your abilities. Remember, I'll be rooting for you and supporting you no matter what."

Building trust through open communication is a gradual process that requires patience. It's important to be patient with each other's communication styles and to recognize that growth and progress take time.

If challenges persist or past traumas affect the relationship, it may be beneficial to seek the guidance of a couples therapist. A trained professional can help facilitate constructive communication and provide valuable insights for building trust.

In conclusion, open and honest communication is the foundation of trust in a romantic relationship. By being transparent, respectful, and empathetic, partners can create a strong bond of trust that fosters a more intimate and fulfilling connection.

Building Trust

In any love relationship, trust is the cornerstone that cements the bond between partners. Building and maintaining trust requires consistent effort and genuine honesty.

Be Reliable and Consistent

One of the most important ways to build trust is to be reliable and consistent. When you make commitments and promises to your partner, keep them. For example, if you agree to do certain household chores, make sure you do them as promised. This reliability shows your partner that he or she can count on you to keep your word and that you are dependable.

Consistency in both actions and words is crucial to building trust. For example, if you express love and affection to your partner, make sure your actions reflect those feelings. Consistency helps reassure your partner that your words are genuine, leading to a stronger sense of trust in the relationship.

Reliability goes beyond fulfilling obligations; it also includes being emotionally available and supportive. For example, if your partner is facing a difficult situation at work or in his or her personal life, be there to listen and offer support. Being consistently present in both good times and challenging moments helps create a sense of security and reassurance that fosters trust.

Avoid Deception

Trust cannot thrive in an environment of deception. Honesty is the foundation of trust in any relationship. Be honest with your partner and avoid withholding important information. For example, if you made a mistake or forgot to tell your partner something important, be upfront about it. Hiding information can lead to a breach of trust, while honest communication strengthens it.

Partner A: "I want to talk about what happened last week when we had that argument. I felt hurt by some of the things you said."

Partner B: "I'm sorry for my part in the argument. I didn't mean to hurt you, and I'm willing to work on my communication to avoid such situations in the future."

Empathy plays an important role in fostering open communication. Putting ourselves in our partner's shoes and trying to understand their feelings and point of view helps build emotional connection and a deeper sense of trust.

Partner A: "I'm nervous about the job interview tomorrow. I really want to get this job."

Partner B: "I understand how important this is for you. You've prepared well, and I have confidence in your abilities. Remember, I'll be rooting for you and supporting you no matter what."

Building trust through open communication is a gradual process that requires patience. It's important to be patient with each other's communication styles and to recognize that growth and progress take time.

If challenges persist or past traumas affect the relationship, it may be beneficial to seek the guidance of a couples therapist. A trained professional can help facilitate constructive communication and provide valuable insights for building trust.

In conclusion, open and honest communication is the foundation of trust in a romantic relationship. By being transparent, respectful, and empathetic, partners can create a strong bond of trust that fosters a more intimate and fulfilling connection.

Building Trust

In any love relationship, trust is the cornerstone that cements the bond between partners. Building and maintaining trust requires consistent effort and genuine honesty.

Be Reliable and Consistent

One of the most important ways to build trust is to be reliable and consistent. When you make commitments and promises to your partner, keep them. For example, if you agree to do certain household chores, make sure you do them as promised. This reliability shows your partner that he or she can count on you to keep your word and that you are dependable.

Consistency in both actions and words is crucial to building trust. For example, if you express love and affection to your partner, make sure your actions reflect those feelings. Consistency helps reassure your partner that your words are genuine, leading to a stronger sense of trust in the relationship.

Reliability goes beyond fulfilling obligations; it also includes being emotionally available and supportive. For example, if your partner is facing a difficult situation at work or in his or her personal life, be there to listen and offer support. Being consistently present in both good times and challenging moments helps create a sense of security and reassurance that fosters trust.

Avoid Deception

Trust cannot thrive in an environment of deception. Honesty is the foundation of trust in any relationship. Be honest with your partner and avoid withholding important information. For example, if you made a mistake or forgot to tell your partner something important, be upfront about it. Hiding information can lead to a breach of trust, while honest communication strengthens it.

Addressing past breaches of trust honestly and openly is critical to rebuilding trust. If trust has been broken in the past, initiate a sincere conversation with your partner. Acknowledge the hurt your actions may have caused and express genuine remorse. For example, if you were not honest about an expense, discuss it openly and take responsibility for your actions. Show your commitment to change and make amends, demonstrating that you are committed to rebuilding trust.

In addition to being honest and reliable, trust is also built through active listening and understanding. Show empathy for your partner's feelings and concerns. For example, if your partner is upset about a difficult day at work, listen carefully and offer comfort and support. Demonstrating that you genuinely care about their well-being and are willing to make an effort to understand them fosters a deeper sense of trust and emotional connection.

Building trust is an ongoing journey that requires consistent effort, vulnerability, and open communication. Trust is delicate and can be easily broken, but when nurtured and respected, it is the foundation of a strong and meaningful relationship. By being reliable and consistent in your actions, and by maintaining a policy of openness and truthfulness, you lay the foundation for a deep and lasting bond built on trust. Remember that trust is a two-way street, and both partners must actively contribute to its growth and maintenance. When trust is present, it paves the way for a relationship filled with love, security, and a shared sense of emotional intimacy.

Developing Emotional Intimacy

Emotional intimacy, the heart of a fulfilling romantic relationship, flourishes when partners create a deep and meaningful connection. This connection is built by sharing experiences and emotions, and by demonstrating genuine empathy and understanding for one another.

Share Experiences and Emotions

To foster emotional intimacy, engage in activities that promote emotional connection and shared experiences. For example, consider taking a leisurely walk hand-in-hand through a nearby park where you can talk about your day, dreams, and aspirations. Or plan a cozy evening at home, cooking your favorite meal together and enjoying the joy of teamwork in the kitchen. These shared experiences create lasting memories and strengthen the bond between partners.

Being emotionally available and receptive is essential to fostering intimacy. Picture this: your partner sits down to share a challenging day at work, and you set aside your phone and distractions to give them your full attention. As they talk, you listen intently, offering words of comfort and nods of understanding. By being emotionally present, you encourage your partner to open up and trust that their feelings are valued and appreciated.

Practice empathy

Empathy, a powerful catalyst for emotional intimacy, involves understanding your partner's feelings and perspective, even if they are different from your own. Let's say your partner is stressed about an upcoming event. You put yourself in their shoes and try to understand their worries and concerns. By acknowledging and reassuring their feelings, you create a safe space for vulnerability and emotional sharing.

Show empathy, even if you do not fully agree with your partner's feelings or opinions. Consider a situation where you disagree on an issue. Instead of dismissing their feelings, express genuine interest in their perspective and try to understand their underlying emotions. This empathic response promotes emotional safety and encourages open communication, allowing both partners to feel accepted and understood.

Practicing empathy also means being sensitive to your partner's needs during difficult times. Imagine your partner facing a difficult situation; you offer a comforting hug and a listening ear. By showing genuine concern and offering support, you strengthen the emotional connection and let your partner know that they can count on you in both good and difficult times.

Patience is essential in developing emotional intimacy. Allow the connection to grow naturally, nurtured by the trust and vulnerability of both partners. By sharing experiences and feelings, actively listening, and practicing empathy, you create a safe and nurturing environment for emotional intimacy to flourish.

Remember that emotional intimacy is an ongoing journey of mutual understanding and connection. As you deepen this intimacy, you build a solid foundation for a loving and fulfilling relationship. Both partners feel genuinely seen, heard, and deeply cared for, resulting in a bond strengthened by love, trust, and authentic emotional connection. Embracing emotional intimacy enriches your relationship, making it a source of comfort, support, and joy.

Cultivating Vulnerability

Vulnerability, the art of allowing ourselves to be seen in our truest form, is a profound gateway to deepening emotional intimacy and trust in a romantic relationship. It involves sharing our inner world, our fears, insecurities, and dreams with our partner, creating an emotional space of authenticity and acceptance.

Share Your Inner World

To cultivate vulnerability, take gradual steps to open up to your partner about your fears, insecurities, and dreams. Imagine sitting together, feeling the warmth of your partner's presence, and mustering the courage to reveal a fear that has lingered in the depths of your heart. As you share, you notice your partner's gentle nod of understanding and the warmth of their touch, creating a sense of safety and acceptance.

Sharing your inner world allows your partner to see the vulnerable parts of you and fosters a deeper emotional connection. It communicates that you trust them with your deepest feelings, fears, and desires. As you both become more comfortable sharing these vulnerabilities, the bond between you grows stronger, laying the foundation for a relationship built on authenticity and mutual understanding.

Accept and Support Each Other

Embracing vulnerability goes hand in hand with accepting and supporting each other unconditionally. Accept your partner as he or she is, with both strengths and weaknesses. Picture a moment when your partner reveals a vulnerability and you respond with open arms and a warm smile, reassuring them that they are loved for who they truly are.

Supporting each other through difficult times is an essential aspect of vulnerability. When your partner faces challenges, be a pillar of emotional support, offering a listening ear, a shoulder to lean on, and words of encouragement. By showing empathy and understanding, you strengthen the emotional bond and create an environment where both partners feel safe to be vulnerable and seek comfort in each other's presence.

In addition to being supportive during difficult times, celebrate each other's successes. Witnessing your partner's accomplishments and sharing in their joy fosters emotional intimacy and strengthens your sense of togetherness. Celebrate their triumphs, large and small, with genuine enthusiasm and pride, knowing that their happiness is intertwined with yours.

Cultivating vulnerability is a transformative journey that requires patience, courage, and a genuine desire to connect deeply with your partner. As you gradually share your inner world and accept each other's vulnerability, you build a relationship that thrives on openness and authenticity. Vulnerability becomes a precious gift that fosters the emotional intimacy and trust that are the foundation of a loving and lasting partnership.

Consider that vulnerability is a reciprocal experience. By sharing and accepting vulnerability with care and compassion, both partners nurture emotional closeness, allowing the relationship to blossom into a space of unwavering love and acceptance. Embracing vulnerability elevates your connection to a higher level where the essence of your true self is celebrated, cherished, and woven into a beautiful weave of emotional intimacy.

Prioritizing Emotional and Physical Intimacy

In a fulfilling romantic relationship, both emotional and physical intimacy are crucial elements that contribute to the depth and connection between partners. By prioritizing these aspects, couples can cultivate a deep bond that includes emotional fulfillment and genuine physical affection.

Physical Affection

Physical affection serves as a tender and expressive language of love that speaks volumes through simple gestures. Whether it's a warm, comforting hug after a long day or a gentle exchange of kisses, physical touch has the power to strengthen the emotional connection between partners.

Through physical affection, couples can express their love, care, and support for each other. Loving touch conveys a sense of security and trust, creating an environment where both partners feel safe to be vulnerable and emotionally open.

The warmth of physical closeness fosters a deep sense of connection, further strengthening the emotional bond between two people.

Physical intimacy goes beyond romantic passion; it encompasses a wide range of affectionate expressions. Simple acts like cuddling on the couch while watching a movie or holding hands on a walk can be just as powerful in enhancing emotional closeness. These moments of physical connection become a reflection of the emotional intimacy nurtured within the relationship, deepening the love and understanding between partners.

It's important to recognize that physical intimacy is intimately connected to emotional intimacy. When emotional closeness is nurtured, physical affection naturally becomes an extension of that bond. Each touch carries the weight of shared experience, trust, and vulnerability, reinforcing the unique connection between partners.

Prioritizing physical affection not only strengthens the emotional connection, but also contributes to overall well-being. Physical touch has been shown to release oxytocin, often called the "love hormone," which promotes feelings of attachment and bonding. This biological response helps to create a strong emotional bond that increases feelings of love, safety, and comfort in the relationship.

However, it's vital to approach physical intimacy with mutual respect and consent. Prioritizing emotional and physical intimacy means being attuned to your partner's needs and boundaries. Open communication about desires and comfort levels ensures that both partners feel respected and valued in every interaction.

By prioritizing emotional and physical intimacy, couples build a relationship that thrives on emotional fulfillment and genuine affection. Through tender physical touch and understanding the unique language of physical intimacy, they cultivate a deep and meaningful connection that weaves together love, trust, and vulnerability.

Prioritizing Emotional and Physical Intimacy

Emotional Intimacy in the Bedroom

The bedroom holds a special place in a romantic relationship, not only as a space for physical intimacy, but also as an opportunity to deepen emotional closeness between partners. By fostering emotional intimacy during intimate moments, couples can create a sacred space where trust, vulnerability, and love intertwine, strengthening their bond in a unique and meaningful way.

Being present and attentive to each other's needs is a cornerstone of emotional intimacy in the bedroom. Imagine a moment when you and your partner have dedicated time for each other, without distractions or worries. As you come together, you focus solely on each other, savoring the moment and the connection you share. By being fully present, you create a sense of safety and connection that makes your partner feel seen, valued, and appreciated.

During intimate moments, communication plays a vital role in fostering emotional intimacy. Honest and open discussions about desires, boundaries, and preferences are essential for a fulfilling and respectful sexual relationship. For example, partners can talk about what brings them pleasure and comfort during intimate encounters. They might discuss any boundaries they have to ensure that both feel comfortable and respected in their vulnerability. These conversations foster trust and understanding, and lay the groundwork for a more intimate and fulfilling sexual experience.

In the bedroom, emotional intimacy also involves acknowledging and validating each other's feelings and emotions. Consider a scenario in which one partner expresses vulnerability or uncertainty about trying something new. The other partner responds with reassurance and tenderness, creating a supportive and nurturing atmosphere. This empathic response strengthens the emotional bond, making the bedroom a place of vulnerability, safety, and mutual satisfaction.

By being emotionally available and responsive, partners can create a deeper connection that goes beyond physical pleasure. Emotional intimacy enhances the sexual experience by creating a deep sense of closeness and trust, making the bedroom a sanctuary of vulnerability and mutual satisfaction.

Keep in mind that emotional intimacy in the bedroom is an ongoing journey of exploration and growth. When you prioritize emotional and physical connection, you cultivate a relationship that thrives on understanding, compassion, and love. By fostering emotional intimacy during intimate moments and having open discussions about desires and boundaries, you create a sacred and cherished space that celebrates the uniqueness of your connection.

Finally, embracing emotional intimacy in the bedroom enriches your connection by making it a haven of trust and vulnerability. By being present, communicative, and emotionally responsive, you foster a sexual relationship that goes beyond physical gratification and brings you closer together as emotionally connected partners. Prioritizing emotional intimacy in the bedroom is a celebration of your love and devotion, creating a deeper and more meaningful bond that transcends the boundaries of the physical world.

Trust, intimacy, and vulnerability are the foundation of a strong and fulfilling relationship.

- Trust: It can be hard to build trust if you have a history of insecure attachment. But you can create a safe space for your partner by being open and honest, and by resolving conflict in a constructive way.

- Intimacy: Emotional intimacy means sharing your experiences and feelings with your partner. You can do this by being emotionally present for each other, supporting each other, and respecting each other's boundaries.

- Vulnerability: Vulnerability is the willingness to be open and honest with your partner, even when it's scary. It's important to be vulnerable in order to build trust and intimacy.

In the next chapter, we will talk about how to become a secure base for each other.

A secure base is a partner who you can rely on for support and comfort. You can become a secure base by being there for your partner when they need you, and by helping them to feel safe and loved.

Let's continue this journey together and discover the joys of becoming a secure base in your romantic relationship.

Chapter 11: Cultivating a Secure Base in Relationships

Understanding the Concept of a Secure Base

In the complex network of human relationships, the concept of a secure base plays a central role in fostering emotional well-being and intimacy. Based on the pioneering work of attachment theory, the idea of a secure base stems from the profound connection that is formed between an infant and his or her primary caregiver. Just as the caregiver provides a safe and nurturing haven for the child to explore the world, a secure base in adult relationships is a sanctuary of love and support that allows both partners to flourish individually and together.

At its core, a secure base is a refuge-a place where partners can seek comfort and protection in times of need or vulnerability. In this nurturing environment, emotional wounds find healing and fears are soothed by the gentle touch of unconditional love. Secure Base partners offer a compassionate ear, a supportive shoulder and an empathetic heart, creating a space where their loved ones feel seen, heard and accepted.

In the embrace of a safe base, personal growth and self-exploration thrive. Just as a young child fearlessly explores her surroundings knowing that her caregiver is nearby, adult partners feel emboldened to take on life's challenges and pursue their aspirations with the assurance that they can always return to the warmth of their partner's affection. This secure attachment fosters resilience and self-confidence, allowing individuals to venture into the unknown with greater courage, knowing they have a firm anchor to keep them grounded.

In addition, a secure base fosters a deep sense of emotional security and trust within the relationship. Partners can rely on each other in times of need, knowing that their vulnerabilities will be met with understanding and care. This trust provides the foundation for intimacy and the basis for open communication, honest expression, and the freedom to be authentic without fear of rejection.

Becoming each Other's Secure Base

The journey of transforming an insecure attachment style into a secure one involves a shared commitment between partners to become each other's secure base. While it may not happen overnight, the process of cultivating a secure base is a profound and transformative endeavor that enriches the relationship and the lives of both individuals involved.

Mirror Exercise

The Mirror Exercise is a powerful tool for strengthening emotional attunement and deepening the connection between partners in a relationship. It involves sitting facing each other and taking turns mirroring each other's facial expressions and body language. By engaging in this exercise, couples can increase their understanding of each other's emotions, improve communication, and cultivate a more secure emotional bond. The exercise is designed to create a safe and intimate space in which partners can develop a heightened awareness of nonverbal cues, fostering a deeper sense of emotional closeness.

To begin the Mirror Exercise, find a quiet and comfortable place where both partners can sit facing each other. Follow these steps to complete the exercise:

a. Set the scene: Eliminate distractions and create a relaxed environment where both partners can focus on each other.

b. Choose the initiator: Decide who will be the initiator for the first round of the exercise. The initiator will begin by nonverbally expressing a simple emotion, such as happiness, sadness, surprise, or curiosity.

c. Mirror and observe: Once the initiator displays the emotion, the other partner mirrors the expression or body language as closely as possible. Observe each other's gestures, facial expressions, and body movements.

d. Switch roles: After a short period of mirroring, switch roles. The partner who mirrored the emotion in the first round now becomes the initiator and the exercise continues.

e. Explore different emotions: Gradually move to displaying a wider range of emotions during the exercise. Experiment with more complex emotions, allowing partners to mirror and attune to each other's emotional states.

f. Communication breaks: Take short breaks after each round to discuss the experience. Share how it felt to be mirrored and how accurately you perceived your partner's emotions. Use this time to express any insights or emotions that arose during the exercise.

Additional tips

a. Be patient and open: The mirroring exercise may feel uncomfortable or awkward at first, especially if you are not used to expressing emotions nonverbally. Approach the exercise with patience and an open mind, allowing yourselves to grow and adapt together.

b. Stay present: During the exercise, focus on the present moment and your partner's nonverbal cues. Avoid distractions or preconceived notions and be fully present with each other.

c. Use a gentle touch: When mirroring body language, consider incorporating gentle touch to strengthen the emotional connection. Holding hands or placing a hand on the other person's shoulder can increase the feeling of intimacy.

d. Practice regularly: Like any skill, emotional attunement improves with practice. Set aside dedicated time to practice the mirror exercise regularly, with the goal of deepening your emotional connection over time.

The Mirror Exercise offers couples a unique and insightful journey toward emotional attunement and connection. Through this exercise, partners can develop a greater understanding of each other's emotions and nonverbal cues, fostering a safe and intimate bond. As you embark on this journey together, remember that emotional attunement is an ongoing process, and the more you practice, the deeper and richer your emotional connection can become. Approach this exercise with curiosity, openness, and a willingness to grow as individuals and as a united and secure couple.

The Appreciation Letters

The Appreciation Letters exercise is a heartfelt and meaningful way for couples to express gratitude and appreciation for each other's unique qualities, thoughtful actions, and gestures that foster feelings of security and love. This exercise is designed to strengthen emotional intimacy by creating a safe and open space where partners can openly communicate their feelings of appreciation. By writing and exchanging these letters, couples can foster a deeper emotional connection and reinforce positive feelings, leading to a more secure and fulfilling relationship.

To begin the Appreciation Letters exercise, follow these steps to create a memorable and emotional experience:

a. Choose the right time: Find a time when both partners can be fully present and undistracted. It could be a special occasion or simply a quiet moment when you can devote your attention solely to this exercise.

b. Set the mood: Create a warm and comfortable environment conducive to sharing feelings of appreciation and vulnerability. Dim the lights, play soft music, or light a candle to create a relaxed atmosphere.

c. Reflect on specific qualities and gestures: Each partner takes time to reflect on the specific qualities, actions, or gestures of the other that have made them feel safe and loved. Be as specific and detailed as possible in your reflections.

d. Write the letter: Each partner writes a heartfelt letter to the other expressing appreciation. Use descriptive language and share personal anecdotes to illustrate the impact these gestures or qualities have had on your emotional well-being.

e. Exchange and read aloud: After writing the letters, share them with each other. Take turns reading the letters aloud, with the writer sharing his or her feelings of appreciation directly with his or her partner.

f. Embrace emotional vulnerability: As you read the letters, allow yourselves to be emotionally vulnerable. Feelings of warmth, joy, and even tears are all natural responses as you give and receive heartfelt appreciation.

g. Reflect and Discuss: After reading both letters, take time to reflect on the experience together. Share how the exercise made you feel and discuss any new insights into each other's emotional needs.

Additional Tips

a. Be sincere and specific: When writing the letters, be sincere and specific in expressing your appreciation. Avoid general statements and instead focus on unique qualities and actions that touched your heart.

b. Practice active listening: As the letters are read, practice active listening by giving your full attention and being fully present. This will strengthen the emotional connection and validate the importance of the exercise.

c. Avoid judgment or criticism: Create a safe and non-judgmental space where both partners can express their feelings without fear of criticism. Remember that appreciation is about recognizing the positive aspects of your partner, not finding fault.

d. Make it a regular practice: While this exercise can be a transformative experience on its own, consider making it a regular practice. Set aside time periodically to express appreciation and gratitude to keep the emotional connection strong.

The Appreciation Letters exercise is a beautiful and transformative journey that allows couples to express genuine gratitude and appreciation for each other's qualities and actions that contribute to feelings of security and love. Through heartfelt letters and active listening, partners can strengthen emotional intimacy and foster a deeper sense of emotional connection and understanding. By making this exercise a regular practice, couples can continue to strengthen their emotional bond and create a more secure and fulfilling relationship. Approach this exercise with honesty, vulnerability, and a willingness to celebrate the unique qualities that make your relationship truly special.

Shared Values and Goals

The Shared Values and Goals Exercise is an important process that allows couples to explore and discuss their shared values, beliefs, and long-term goals. By taking the time to identify areas of agreement and shared goals, partners can strengthen their sense of security and commitment to the relationship. This exercise creates a space for open communication and fosters a deeper understanding of each other's hopes and dreams. Knowing that you both share similar values and have common goals can build a strong foundation of trust and unity, enhancing the overall health and stability of the relationship.

Follow these practical steps to effectively implement the Shared Values and Goals Exercise:

a. Set aside dedicated time: Find a time when both partners can have meaningful discussions without distractions or time constraints. Choose a relaxed environment that allows for open and honest communication.

b. Initiate an open dialogue: Begin the conversation by expressing the importance of this exercise and your desire to explore your shared values and aspirations together. Emphasize that this is a collaborative effort to strengthen your connection as a couple.

c. Identify core values: Begin by individually listing your core values and beliefs. These may include aspects related to family, personal growth, career, spirituality, community involvement, or lifestyle preferences.

d. Share and discuss: Share your lists and take turns discussing the values that are most important to you. Be open to sharing personal stories or experiences that have shaped these values. Actively listen to each other's perspectives and seek to understand each other.

e. Explore long-term goals: Move on to discussing your long-term goals as individuals and as a couple. These goals can cover various aspects of life, such as career, finances, family planning, travel, personal development, and more.

f. Identify common goals: Look for areas of alignment where your individual goals overlap to form common goals. Highlight those goals that resonate with both partners and are important to your journey together.

g. Create an action plan: Once shared goals are identified, work together to create an action plan for achieving them. Break down the goals into smaller, achievable steps and discuss the roles each partner can play in the process.

Additional Tips

a. Embrace differences: While identifying shared values and goals is essential, it is also natural for partners to have some differences in their individual aspirations. Embrace these differences and see them as opportunities to grow and learn from each other.

b. Regular check-ins: As life evolves, goals and values may change. Schedule regular check-ins to reassess your shared values and goals to ensure that you stay on the same page and continue to support each other's aspirations.

c. Be supportive: Encourage each other to pursue individual and shared goals and dreams. Supporting your partner's personal growth and aspirations will foster a sense of security and trust in the relationship.

d. Celebrate milestones: Celebrate the achievement of shared goals and milestones along the way. Acknowledging the progress made together will build a sense of accomplishment and teamwork.

The Shared Values and Goals exercise is a powerful tool for couples to build a strong sense of security, unity, and commitment. By exploring shared values, discussing long-term goals, and setting goals together, partners can deepen their understanding of each other and create a solid foundation for their future together. Approach the process with an open heart, active listening, and a genuine desire to support and nurture each other's dreams. The exercise will undoubtedly lead to a more harmonious and fulfilling relationship where both partners feel supported, understood, and connected on a deep level.

Conflict Resolution Practice

The Conflict Resolution Practice is a transformative exercise that equips couples with effective tools to manage disagreements and conflict in a constructive way. Every relationship encounters conflict, but how partners approach and resolve it can have a significant impact on the overall health and harmony of the relationship. This exercise is designed to promote open communication, active listening, and empathy during conflict. By practicing a structured approach to conflict resolution, couples can foster deeper understanding, strengthen emotional bonds, and work together to find compromises and solutions that satisfy both partners.

Follow these practical steps to implement conflict resolution practice in your relationship:

a. Create a peaceful environment: Choose a neutral and calm space to engage in conflict resolution. Minimize distractions and ensure that both partners can focus solely on the discussion at hand.

b. Agree on the structure: Before beginning the training, agree on the structure for conflict resolution. Decide who will have the floor and establish guidelines such as no interruptions, no personal attacks, and no raising of voices.

c. Take turns speaking: When a conflict arises, designate one partner to begin by expressing his or her perspective calmly and honestly. The other partner listens carefully without interrupting or interjecting.

d. Active Listening: The listening partner should actively listen to understand his or her partner's point of view. After the first partner has finished speaking, the listener may paraphrase and repeat what he or she has heard to ensure clarity and to show empathy.

e. Switch roles: Once the first partner has expressed his or her perspective, switch roles. The listener becomes the speaker, expressing his or her point of view, while the other partner actively listens and practices paraphrasing.

f. Seek Common Ground: After both partners have expressed their perspectives, focus on identifying areas of agreement and shared interests. Use these commonalities as a basis for finding compromises and solutions.

g. Brainstorm Solutions: Work together to brainstorm possible solutions to the conflict. Be open to considering different approaches and be willing to make concessions when necessary.

h. Mutual Agreement: Aim for a mutual agreement that takes into account the needs and perspectives of both partners. Avoid a "winner" and "loser" mentality, and instead seek a win-win solution.

Additional Tips

a. Practice patience: Conflict resolution takes time and effort, especially when emotions are running high. Be patient with each other and avoid rushing the process so that both partners feel heard and valued.

b. Choose the right time: Avoid engaging in conflict resolution when either partner is overly tired, stressed, or emotionally overwhelmed. Wait for a time when both of you can approach the discussion with a calmer demeanor.

c. Use "I" statements: When expressing feelings and concerns, use "I" statements to convey how specific actions or situations affect you personally. This approach avoids sounding accusatory and promotes understanding.

d. Learn from conflict: View conflict as an opportunity for growth and learning in the relationship. Embrace conflict as a chance to better understand each other's needs and strengthen your bond.

The practice of conflict resolution offers couples a structured and empathetic approach to resolving disagreements and conflict. By actively listening, calmly expressing perspectives, and working together toward solutions, partners can cultivate a relationship based on effective communication and mutual respect. By embracing conflict as a path to growth and understanding, couples can create a harmonious and resilient bond that meets challenges with grace. Regularly practicing conflict resolution strengthens emotional connections, making the relationship a haven of support, understanding, and love.

Emotional Check-ins

Emotional check-ins are a powerful practice designed to foster emotional intimacy and strengthen the emotional connection between partners. This exercise involves scheduling regular moments of vulnerability where each partner takes turns sharing their feelings and emotional experiences from the past week. The goal is to create a safe and supportive space for open communication, active listening, and empathetic understanding. By engaging in emotional check-ins, couples can develop a deeper understanding of each other's emotional landscapes, provide validation and support, and cultivate a relationship based on emotional closeness and trust.

Follow these practical steps to effectively implement Emotional Check-ins in your relationship:

a. Set a consistent time: Agree on a regular time for Emotional Check-ins that works for both partners' schedules. It could be once a week or more often, depending on what works best for you as a couple.

b. Create a safe space: Find a private and comfortable space where you both feel comfortable and can share openly without distractions or interruptions.

c. Take turns sharing: During each emotional check-in, designate one partner to be the speaker and the other to be the listener. The speaker has the floor to share his or her feelings and emotional experiences from the past week.

d. Active Listening: As the listener, practice active listening by giving your full attention to your partner. Avoid interrupting or jumping in with immediate advice. Instead, focus on understanding their feelings and experiences.

e. Empathetic Responses: As a listener, respond with empathy and affirmation. Express understanding and support for your partner's feelings without judgment.

f. Switch roles: After the speaker has shared his or her feelings, switch roles and let the listener become the speaker. Continue the practice, alternating between sharing and listening.

g. Avoid problem-solving: Emotional check-ins are not about solving problems; they are about creating a safe space for emotional expression and understanding. Focus on validating each other's feelings rather than offering immediate solutions.

Additional tips

a. Practice vulnerability: Emotional check-ins may feel challenging at first, especially if you are not used to sharing emotions openly. Embrace vulnerability and take gradual steps toward sharing deeper feelings over time.

b. Be non-judgmental: Create a judgment-free zone during emotional check-ins. Avoid criticizing or dismissing each other's feelings, as this can hinder emotional intimacy.

c. Express appreciation: After each emotional check-in, take a moment to express appreciation for your partner's openness and willingness to share his or her feelings.

d. Adjust the frequency: Be flexible with the frequency of Emotional Check-ins based on your evolving needs as a couple. If you find that you need more or less frequent check-ins, communicate and adjust accordingly.

Emotional check-ins provide couples with a valuable opportunity to deepen their emotional connection and foster a greater understanding of each other's feelings. By practicing active listening, empathy, and vulnerability, partners can create a safe and supportive space for emotional expression. Engaging in regular emotional check-ins strengthens the emotional bond and paves the way for a more fulfilling and intimate relationship. As you embark on this journey of emotional openness, remember that true emotional intimacy is built on trust, respect, and genuine concern for each other's well-being. Embrace the practice of emotional check-ins with an open heart and watch your emotional connection blossom and enrich the love you share as a couple.

Nurturing Rituals

Nurturing Rituals are a powerful and intentional practice designed to strengthen emotional connection and foster a deeper sense of intimacy in a relationship. These rituals involve setting aside dedicated time for daily or weekly activities that prioritize emotional connection and quality time together. By engaging in Nurturing Rituals, couples create meaningful moments of connection and emotional safety that reinforce their love and commitment to each other. These simple yet profound acts of nurturing can serve as anchors of stability and joy, nourishing the relationship and cultivating a strong and loving bond.

Follow these practical steps to successfully implement Nurturing Rituals in your relationship:

a. Decide on rituals together: As a couple, sit down and discuss what nurturing rituals you would like to establish. Consider activities that promote emotional intimacy, such as technology-free dinners, evening walks, morning coffee together, or designated cuddling time before bed.

b. Schedule the rituals: Agree on a specific schedule for the nurturing rituals. This could be a daily ritual, such as having dinner together, or a weekly ritual, such as going for a walk on Sundays. Consistency is key to making these rituals a meaningful part of your routine.

c. Create a ritual environment: Prepare the environment for your care rituals to ensure a comfortable and inviting space. For example, set the table beautifully for dinner, choose a scenic route for your walk, or create a cozy place to snuggle.

d. Be present and engaged: During nurturing rituals, focus on being fully present and engaged with each other. Put away distractions such as phones or screens and focus your attention on each other.

e. Open communication: Use nurturing rituals as opportunities for open communication. Share your thoughts, feelings, and experiences during these moments of connection, fostering emotional safety and vulnerability.

f. Express Affection: Include moments of physical affection and emotional closeness during rituals. Hold hands, exchange hugs, or share gentle touches to strengthen your emotional connection.

g. Be flexible and adaptable: Life can get busy and unforeseen circumstances can arise. Be flexible and adaptable with your nurturing rituals, adjusting them as needed but prioritizing the connection they foster.

Additional tips

a. Personalize the rituals: Tailor the nurturing rituals to your unique preferences and interests as a couple. Choose activities that resonate with both of you and align with your shared values.

b. Rotate and Explore: Keep your nurturing rituals fresh and exciting by occasionally rotating or exploring new activities. Trying new things together can reinvigorate your emotional connection and create lasting memories.

c. Gratitude and appreciation: Use nurturing rituals as opportunities to express gratitude and appreciation for each other. Celebrate your love and the effort each partner puts into the relationship.

d. Overcome challenges together: When conflicts or challenges arise, use the nurturing rituals as a space to work through them and support each other emotionally. These moments of connection can be especially powerful in times of difficulty.

Nurturing rituals offer couples an invaluable opportunity to prioritize emotional connection and intimacy in their relationship. By creating daily or weekly moments of connection, partners can strengthen their love, commitment, and emotional security. Engaging in nurturing rituals fosters a deep and lasting emotional connection, enhancing the overall well-being and happiness of the relationship. As you embark on this journey of intentional connection, remember that the small acts of love and care in nurturing rituals have the power to make a significant impact on the strength and longevity of your relationship. Embrace these nurturing rituals with joy and enthusiasm and watch your emotional connection blossom and enrich the love you share as a couple.

Saying I Love You in Different Ways

The practice of saying "I love you" in different ways is a beautiful and enriching exercise that encourages couples to express love and affection in different and creative ways. While saying "I love you" is deeply meaningful, incorporating various acts of kindness, surprises, and thoughtful gestures can enhance feelings of security and care within the relationship. This exercise is designed to foster a deeper emotional connection by nurturing a sense of love and appreciation through small, meaningful actions. By exploring unique ways to express affection, partners can strengthen their bond and create a love that is felt through both words and actions.

Follow these practical steps to implement the "Saying I Love You in Different Ways" exercise:

a. Set intentions together: As a couple, discuss the purpose and meaning of the exercise. Acknowledge that expressing love in different ways goes beyond words and is an opportunity to show affection and appreciation in creative and thoughtful ways.

b. Brainstorm ideas: Spend time together brainstorming different ways to express love. Consider both grand and simple gestures, such as surprise gifts, love notes, acts of service, planning a special date night, or offering a warm hug during difficult moments.

c. Surprise each other: Embrace the element of surprise by occasionally doing these gestures unexpectedly. Little surprises in everyday life can bring joy and strengthen the emotional connection.

d. Be observant and thoughtful: Pay attention to your partner's preferences, desires, and love language. Tailor your expressions of love to what resonates most deeply with your partner.

e. Celebrate special occasions: Use special occasions such as birthdays, anniversaries, or milestones to express love in meaningful ways. Thoughtful gestures on these occasions can make them even more memorable and appreciated.

f. Create a love jar or scrapbook: Consider starting a love jar or scrapbook together. Fill the jar with written notes expressing love and appreciation, or create a scrapbook that documents cherished memories and moments of affection.

g. Open and honest communication: Encourage open communication about how each partner best receives and appreciates expressions of love. This understanding will help tailor gestures to be more meaningful and effective.

Additional tips

a. Be genuine and spontaneous: Make sure expressions of love are genuine and from the heart. Let spontaneity guide some gestures, as they can have a special charm.

b. Avoid comparison: Each expression of love is unique and meaningful in its own way. Avoid comparing gestures, as this can diminish the authenticity and sincerity behind them.

c. Embrace Reciprocity: Encourage a culture of reciprocal gestures in the relationship. Both partners can participate in expressing love in different ways, fostering a cycle of affection and care.

d. Continue to grow and explore: Love is an ever-evolving journey, so continue to explore new ways of expressing affection and appreciation throughout your relationship.

Saying "I love you" in different ways is a heartwarming and transformative exercise that enhances emotional connection and deepens the bond between partners. By expressing love through various acts of kindness, surprises, and thoughtful gestures, couples can cultivate a love that is felt in both words and actions. Approach this exercise with creativity, sincerity, and spontaneity, and watch your relationship blossom with a deeper sense of love, security, and care. As you embark on this journey of diverse expressions of love, remember that each act, no matter how small, has the power to strengthen your emotional connection and make your love story even more extraordinary.

Vision for the Future

The Vision for the Future exercise is a transformative practice that invites couples to embark on a journey to envision their life together. By openly discussing both short-term and long-term goals, partners can create a shared vision for their future as a couple. This exercise fosters deeper emotional connection, mutual understanding, and a sense of purpose in the relationship. By exploring hopes and dreams as a team, couples can strengthen their bond, align their ambitions, and create a path to a fulfilling and unified future.

Follow these practical steps to effectively implement the Visioning exercise:

a. Find a quiet and private setting: Set aside time in a quiet and private setting where both partners can have a meaningful discussion without distractions.

b. Initiate the conversation: Open the conversation by expressing the importance of discussing your vision for the future together. Encourage your partner to openly share his or her thoughts and aspirations.

c. Explore short-term goals: Begin by discussing short-term goals and aspirations that you both have for the next few months or years. Share your individual visions and discuss how they align or complement each other.

d. Discuss long-term goals: Continue to explore your long-term goals and dreams as a couple. This can include topics such as career goals, family planning, travel, personal growth, or any other significant life goals.

e. Support each other: Discuss how you can support each other in achieving these goals. Identify areas where you can provide emotional, practical, or financial support to help each other grow.

f. Create a Vision Statement: Together create a vision statement for your future as a couple. This statement should encapsulate your shared dreams and values and serve as a guiding light for your journey together.

g. Set milestones: Break down your long-term goals into smaller, achievable milestones. Set specific goals and celebrate your accomplishments as you progress toward your shared vision.

h. Revisit and adjust: Revisit your vision for the future regularly, especially during significant life events or changes. Be open to adjusting your plans as your journey together unfolds.

Additional tips

a. Be Open and Honest: Commit to open and honest communication throughout the process. Share your feelings, fears, and hopes to foster a deeper emotional connection.

b. Respect individual desires: While working toward a shared vision, respect each other's individual aspirations and dreams. Make room for both shared and personal growth.

c. Embrace Compromise: In cases of differing goals or aspirations, embrace compromise to find solutions that honor the needs and desires of both partners.

d. Practice Active Listening: During the conversation, practice active listening to truly understand each other's perspectives and feelings. Validate your partner's thoughts and feelings with empathy.

The visioning exercise offers couples an invaluable opportunity to create a shared path filled with love, understanding, and mutual support. By discussing short- and long-term goals, partners can foster a deeper connection and build a foundation of shared aspirations. Embrace this exercise with enthusiasm and sincerity, for the journey of envisioning a future together is a beautiful testament to your commitment and love. As you explore your shared vision and support each other's dreams, remember that each step you take together brings you closer to a future filled with happiness, growth, and fulfillment as a united couple.

Gratitude Practice

The Gratitude Practice is a powerful and transformative exercise that cultivates appreciation and promotes positivity in a relationship. By taking a moment each day to express gratitude for something specific about your partner or your relationship, you can strengthen the emotional connection and deepen the bond between you. This practice encourages couples to recognize and acknowledge the positive aspects of each other and their shared journey, fostering a sense of joy, love, and contentment. Embracing the practice of gratitude allows couples to cultivate a culture of appreciation, leading to a more harmonious and fulfilling relationship.

Follow these practical steps to effectively implement the practice of gratitude in your relationship:

a. Set a daily reminder: Find a consistent time each day to practice gratitude. It could be in the morning, during dinner, or before bed. Set a reminder that prompts you to express your gratitude.

b. Reflect on specific moments: Take a moment to reflect on specific moments, qualities, or actions your partner displayed during the day. It could be something they did to support you, a kind gesture, or a quality you admire.

c. Verbalize your gratitude: Share your gratitude with your partner either in person, in a text message, or in a handwritten note. Be specific about what you appreciate about them or your relationship.

d. Listen with openness: When your partner expresses gratitude, listen with openness and sincerity. Receive their words with warmth and gratitude in return.

e. Rotate and Explore: Keep the practice fresh by expressing gratitude for different aspects of your partner or relationship each day. Explore different aspects of appreciation to deepen your connection.

f. Include Self-Gratitude: Encourage self-gratitude by also taking a moment to appreciate your own actions or qualities that have positively impacted the relationship or your partner.

g. Be sincere and heartfelt: Practice heartfelt gratitude by ensuring that your expressions of appreciation are genuine and heartfelt.

Additional tips

a. Consistency is key: Make gratitude a consistent part of your daily routine. Small acts of gratitude can have a significant impact over time.

b. Focus on effort and intention: Gratitude is not about perfection or grand gestures, but about recognizing the effort and intention behind your partner's actions.

c. Celebrate the little things: Don't overlook the importance of appreciating the little things. Small gestures can carry immense meaning and contribute to a positive atmosphere.

d. Keep a Gratitude Journal: Consider keeping a shared gratitude journal to document each other's expressions of gratitude. This can become a treasured memento of your journey together.

The practice of gratitude is a beautiful and transformative exercise that enriches the emotional connection and fosters a culture of appreciation in your relationship. By expressing daily gratitude for specific moments, qualities, or actions, couples can deepen their love, joy, and sense of contentment. Embrace this practice with sincerity, warmth, and openness, and watch your relationship blossom with a deeper appreciation for each other. As you cultivate gratitude and positivity, remember that this simple yet profound practice has the power to infuse your relationship with a lasting sense of love, happiness, and emotional closeness.

In this chapter, we talked about how to become a secure base in a relationship.

- Emotional intimacy: This means being open and honest with your partner, and sharing your feelings.

- Trust: This means feeling safe and secure with your partner, and knowing that they will be there for you.

- Vulnerability: This means being willing to let your partner see your true self, even when it's scary.

We also talked about some exercises and techniques that can help you become a secure base in your relationship.

- The mirror exercise: This is a visualization exercise that can help you see yourself more positively.

- Appreciation letters: These are letters that you write to your partner expressing your gratitude for them.

- Conflict resolution practice: This is a way to learn how to resolve conflict in a healthy way.

- Emotional check-ins: These are regular check-ins with your partner to talk about your feelings and needs.

- Nurturing rituals: These are activities that you do with your partner to connect and build intimacy.

- Saying "I love you" in different ways: This is a way to express your love for your partner in new and creative ways.

- Envisioning the future together: This is a way to talk about your hopes and dreams for the future with your partner.

In the next chapter, we will talk about how to become a secure base for yourself.

This means learning to love and accept yourself, and building a strong sense of self-worth. This is an important journey, whether you are in a relationship or not.

Let's dive into the next chapter and explore the beautiful concept of finding security and happiness within ourselves.

Chapter 12: Becoming Your Own Secure Base: Fostering Self-Love and Unleashing Your Authenticity

Being single doesn't mean you're alone; it means you have the freedom to focus on yourself. It's a time in your life when you can prioritize your own needs, desires, and ambitions without compromise. Instead of seeing singleness as a void to be filled, embrace it as an opportunity to cultivate a deeper connection with the most important person in your life - yourself!

During this time, you have the chance to delve deeper into your passions, interests, and dreams. Explore what truly brings you joy and fulfillment. Whether it's pursuing a hobby, learning a new skill, or embarking on an adventure, this is your time to shine. Embrace the excitement of self-discovery and watch your confidence soar to new heights.

Just remember that the relationship you build with yourself is just as important as any other. In fact, it's the foundation for all your future relationships. When you love and value yourself, you set the standard for how others should treat you. So take the time to understand your wants and needs, and don't be afraid to set healthy boundaries in your relationships.

Being single is not a limitation; it's an opportunity for solo growth! It's a chance to work on becoming the best version of yourself - a person who is content, fulfilled, and independent. Use this time to invest in your personal growth, both emotionally and intellectually. Read those books you've always wanted to read, take that class you've been curious about, or simply spend quality time with yourself, reflecting on your journey and your goals.

Accepting your single status gives you the strength to make independent decisions and chart your own course in life. You're not bound by anyone else's expectations or demands, giving you the freedom to explore and experiment with different aspects of your life. This is the perfect opportunity to grow into the person you want to be without limitations holding you back.

Being single also allows you to develop a healthy relationship with loneliness. Instead of dreading it, embrace the moments of silence and reflection. In these moments, you'll learn to appreciate your own company and find inner peace and tranquility. Solitude becomes a source of strength and creativity from which you can draw inspiration and confidence.

As you begin this path of solitary growth, it's important to stay true to yourself and not rush into a relationship just for the sake of being with someone. Wait for a connection that aligns with your values, ambitions, and passions. Remember, being single is a time for personal growth and self-discovery; it's not a race to find a partner.

Loving Yourself, No Strings Attached

Ah, self-love-a beautiful and transformative journey that begins with giving yourself the gift of unconditional affection. Imagine being your own best friend, the one who stands by you through thick and thin, celebrating your victories and comforting you in moments of uncertainty. That is the essence of unconditional self-love.

To embark on this path, treat yourself with the kindness and compassion you would effortlessly extend to a cherished friend. Acknowledge that you, too, are worthy of love and care. Embrace the idea that self-love is not a selfish act, but a vital form of nurturing your soul.

As you walk this path of self-discovery, remember to celebrate your successes with the same enthusiasm you'd shower on a dear friend. Often we downplay our accomplishments, dismissing them as mere strokes of luck or trivial matters. Instead, let your heart swell with pride and joy at each step forward.

Of course, we all make mistakes-that's an inevitable part of the human experience. But instead of dwelling on your missteps with self-criticism, practice forgiveness. Just as you would forgive a friend's mistakes, extend the same grace to yourself. Recognize that growth comes from learning, and even the most stumbling steps help you progress.

Embrace your imperfections, for they are what make you unique and authentic. We tend to be our own harshest critics, picking apart every flaw and blemish. But think about how you'd react if a friend shared their insecurities with you. You'd probably remind them that those imperfections are what make them special and lovable. Extend the same grace to yourself.

The love you give to yourself should be genuine, unencumbered by conditions or expectations. It's not about earning love or trying to live up to some imagined ideal. It's about recognizing your value as a human being who is inherently worthy of love, compassion, and acceptance.

So go ahead and shower yourself with love, no strings attached! Embrace the beautiful complexity of your being - your quirks, your talents, and your dreams.

Know that you are worthy of love and care, not only from others, but from yourself. Remember that self-love is not a destination; it's an ongoing journey of discovery and growth.

Along the way, you may encounter moments of self-doubt or times when loving yourself feels distant. That's okay; it's all part of the process. Be patient and gentle with yourself as you work through these feelings. Remember that self-love, like any relationship, takes effort, patience, and understanding.

Above all, remember that you are enough just the way you are. Embrace your uniqueness and appreciate the person you are becoming. Love yourself wholeheartedly, without conditions or reservations, and watch that love overflow and touch every aspect of your life. Your heart will blossom and you'll radiate a love so profound that others will be inspired to embark on their own journey of self-love.

Now, let's explore how you can become your own secure base, regardless of whether you are single or in a relationship. Developing a strong connection with yourself is essential for personal growth and well-being. Here are 10 practical steps that I believe are essential to achieving this.

1. Get to know yourself

This means understanding your values, strengths and weaknesses, dreams and goals. It also means understanding your emotions and how you react to different situations. When you know yourself well, you are better able to make decisions that are in your best interests.

- **Values:** What are the things that are most important to you? What do you believe in? Your values are the foundation of your identity, so it is important to take some time to reflect on them.

- **Strengths and weaknesses:** What are you good at? What are you not so good at? Knowing your strengths and weaknesses can help you to set realistic goals and to avoid taking on challenges that are beyond your reach.

- **Dreams and goals:** What do you want to achieve in life? What are your short-term and long-term goals? Having dreams and goals gives you something to strive for and can help you to stay motivated.

- **Emotions:** How do you feel? How do you express your emotions? It is important to be aware of your emotions and to learn how to manage them in a healthy way.

- **Reactions:** How do you react to different situations? Are you typically calm and collected, or do you tend to get stressed out easily? Understanding your reactions can help you to avoid making impulsive decisions and to cope with difficult situations more effectively.

2. Spend time alone

This may seem daunting at first, but it is important to learn to enjoy your own company. When you are alone, you can relax and be yourself without worrying about what others think. Spending time alone can also help you to connect with your inner voice and to discover what you truly want out of life.

Benefits of spending time alone:

- **Increased self-awareness:** When you spend time alone, you have the opportunity to reflect on your thoughts, feelings, and experiences. This can help you to develop a deeper understanding of yourself and your needs.

- **Reduced stress:** Spending time alone can help you to relax and de-stress. This is because you are not bombarded with external stimuli, such as noise and social interaction.

- **Increased creativity:** Spending time alone can help you to tap into your creativity. This is because you are not distracted by others and you have the freedom to explore your thoughts and ideas without judgment.

- **Improved problem-solving skills:** Spending time alone can help you to develop your problem-solving skills. This is because you are forced to think for yourself and to come up with your own solutions.

3. Do things that make you happy

This is an essential part of becoming your own secure base. When you are doing things that make you happy, you are more likely to feel content and fulfilled. This will also help you to build your self-esteem and to feel more confident in yourself.

How to find things that make you happy:

- **Think about what you enjoyed doing as a child.** What activities did you find fun and engaging?

- **Pay attention to what makes you feel good.** What activities make you feel relaxed, energized, or fulfilled?

- **Experiment with new activities.** Try something that you've never done before and see if you enjoy it.

- **Ask your friends and family for suggestions.** They may know of activities that you would enjoy.

4. Take care of yourself

This means eating healthy, exercising, and getting enough sleep. When you are taking care of your physical and mental health, you are better able to cope with stress and challenges. You will also have more energy and be more productive.

How to take care of yourself:

- **Eat a healthy diet.** This means eating plenty of fruits, vegetables, and whole grains.

- **Exercise regularly.** Aim for at least 30 minutes of moderate-intensity exercise most days of the week.

- **Get enough sleep.** Most adults need around 7-8 hours of sleep per night.

- **Manage stress.** There are many different ways to manage stress, such as yoga, meditation, or spending time in nature.

5. Set boundaries

This is important for both your physical and emotional well-being. It means knowing what you are comfortable with and what you are not. It also means being able to say no to things that you don't want to do. When you set boundaries, you are respecting yourself and your needs.

How to set boundaries:

- **Be clear about your needs.** What are you comfortable with and what are you not?

- **Be assertive.** This means being able to say no to things that you don't want to do.

- **Be respectful of others' boundaries.** Just as you deserve to have your boundaries respected, so do others.

- **Be consistent.** If you set a boundary, stick to it. This will help others to understand what you are and are not comfortable with.

6. Be assertive

This means standing up for yourself and your needs. It doesn't mean being aggressive or demanding, but it does mean being able to communicate your wants and needs in a clear and respectful way. When you are assertive, you are more likely to get what you want and need.

How to be assertive:

- **Be direct.** State your needs clearly and directly.

- **Be respectful.** Even if you are saying no to something, do so in a respectful way.

- **Be confident.** Believe in yourself and your ability to get what you want.

- **Be prepared to compromise.** Sometimes, you may need to compromise in order to get what you want.

7. Practice self-compassion

This means being kind and understanding to yourself, even when you make mistakes. Everyone makes mistakes, so don't beat yourself up over them. Self-compassion will help you to be more forgiving of yourself and to move on from mistakes.

How to practice self-compassion:

- **Be aware of your thoughts and feelings.** When you make a mistake, pay attention to how you are talking to yourself.

- **Be kind to yourself.** Talk to yourself the way you would talk to a friend who made a mistake.

- **Focus on the positive.** Instead of dwelling on your mistakes, focus on the things you did well.

- **Be patient with yourself.** It takes time to develop self-compassion.

8. Let go of the past

Holding onto grudges and resentments will only weigh you down. Forgive yourself and others, and move on with your life. Holding onto the past will only prevent you from living in the present moment and enjoying your life.

How to let go of the past:

- **Acknowledge your pain.** It is okay to feel pain, but don't let it consume you.

- **Forgive yourself and others.** This doesn't mean forgetting what happened, but it does mean letting go of the anger and resentment.

- **Focus on the present moment.** The past is over, and you can't change it. But you can choose to live in the present moment and enjoy your life.

9. Live in the present moment

Don't dwell on the past or worry about the future. Focus on the present moment and enjoy the here and now. The present moment is all we have, so make the most of it!

How to live in the present moment:

- **Be aware of your thoughts and feelings.** When you are present, you are aware of what you are thinking and feeling.

- **Pay attention to your surroundings.** Notice the sights, sounds, smells, and sensations around you.

- **Be mindful of your body.** Notice how your body feels, both physically and emotionally.

- **Be grateful for what you have.** Take some time each day to appreciate the good things in your life.

10. Be grateful

Take some time each day to appreciate the good things in your life. Gratitude will help you to focus on the positive and boost your self-esteem. When you are grateful for what you have, you are more likely to be happy and content.

How to be grateful:

- **Keep a gratitude journal.** Each day, write down three things you are grateful for.

- **Practice mindful gratitude.** Take some time each day to focus on the things you are grateful for.

- **Express your gratitude to others.** Let the people in your life know how much you appreciate them.

You are on the path to becoming the best version of yourself, and being a secure base for yourself is an incredible gift. Whether you're single, in a relationship, or navigating the ups and downs of life, remember that you have the strength within you to build a fulfilling and meaningful life based on self-love and authenticity. Embrace this journey wholeheartedly, and watch yourself flourish in ways you never thought possible. You've got this!

Being single can be a time for self-discovery and personal growth.

- Self-love: This means treating yourself with kindness, celebrating your successes, and forgiving your mistakes.

- Self-awareness: This means spending time alone and doing things that bring you joy and fulfillment.

- Boundaries: This means setting healthy boundaries with others and being assertive in your needs.

- Gratitude: This means expressing gratitude daily for the blessings in your life.

In the next chapter, we will talk about how to overcome past trauma and heal the wounds of attachment.

This journey will empower you to become your own secure base, leading to a life of authenticity, fulfillment, and meaningful connections with others.

Chapter 13: Addressing Past Trauma and Attachment Wounds

In previous chapters, we explored attachment theory and the different styles that play a significant role in shaping our relationships and emotional well-being. As mentioned in previous chapters, attachment styles are influenced by early experiences with caregivers and have a profound impact on how we form and maintain bonds with others throughout our lives. However, if these early experiences are negative or traumatic, they can lead to insecure attachment styles and attachment wounds.

Recognize the impact of past experiences on current attachment styles

Attachment styles are not static, but are shaped by our early experiences, especially with caregivers during infancy and childhood. When caregivers are consistently responsive, nurturing, and emotionally available, they promote secure attachment. On the other hand, inconsistent, neglectful, or abusive caregiving can lead to insecure attachment styles, such as anxious, avoidant, or disorganized attachment.

Individuals with insecure attachment styles often carry unresolved emotional wounds from the past. These attachment wounds can manifest in their adult relationships, making it difficult to form healthy and satisfying attachments. For example, those with an anxious attachment style may struggle with an excessive need for reassurance and fear of abandonment, while those with an avoidant attachment style may have difficulty opening up emotionally and forming intimate bonds.

The importance of addressing and healing attachment wounds

Recognizing and understanding one's attachment style and underlying attachment wounds is critical to personal growth and creating healthier relationships. Unresolved attachment wounds can cause distress, anxiety, and even affect mental health and overall well-being. Without addressing these wounds, individuals may inadvertently perpetuate negative patterns in their relationships, creating a cycle of pain and disconnection.

Healing attachment wounds requires a multifaceted approach that may include therapy, self-education, and personal reflection. Here are some important steps in the healing process:

Self-Reflection: Unveiling the Path to Healing Attachment Wounds

Self-reflection is a profound and transformative process that lies at the heart of healing attachment wounds. It enables individuals to delve into their emotional landscape, examine past experiences, and gain valuable insight into the influence of their attachment style on their behavior and emotions in relationships. By shedding light on these internal dynamics, self-reflection becomes a powerful tool for reclaiming emotional well-being and taking ownership of the healing journey.

The essence of self-reflection

Self-reflection is a process of deep introspection in which we become observers of our inner world. It encourages us to approach our thoughts and feelings with non-judgmental curiosity. By becoming more attuned to our emotions and their origins, we can decipher how past experiences have shaped our attachment style and influenced our current relationships. Through self-awareness, we uncover the subtle ways our attachment wounds play out in our interactions, enabling us to break free from repetitive patterns and foster healthier connections.

Uncover early experiences

Self-reflection prompts us to revisit our early experiences with caregivers and how those interactions shaped our attachment style. Delving into our past with a compassionate lens allows us to reconnect with the child we once were. By revisiting our early experiences, we acknowledge the pain and unmet needs we may have experienced. This acknowledgment helps us develop empathy for our younger selves and fosters self-compassion. Understanding the impact of past interactions with caregivers gives us insight into the roots of our attachment style, enabling us to challenge ingrained beliefs and embrace healthier ways of relating to others.

Embrace vulnerability and ownership

Examining attachment wounds can evoke feelings of vulnerability. Embracing vulnerability means allowing ourselves to acknowledge our emotional pain without judgment or self-criticism. Through self-reflection, we begin to see that our attachment wounds do not define us; rather, they are part of our human experience. By taking ownership of our healing journey, we reclaim agency over our emotional well-being and our relationships. We become active participants in our growth, choosing to cultivate healthier attachment patterns and create fulfilling connections with others.

Insights into attachment behaviors

Self-reflection brings attention to the attachment behaviors that have become ingrained in our interactions with others. As we engage in self-reflection, we uncover the unconscious scripts that govern our relationship behaviors. By identifying our attachment responses, we can begin to see how these behaviors may have served as coping mechanisms in the past. Understanding their origins empowers us to challenge and reshape these responses, paving the way for more authentic and secure connections with others.

The role of mindfulness

Mindfulness serves as a gentle anchor that keeps us rooted in the present moment. Through this practice, we develop the ability to observe our emotional responses without being swept away by them. Mindfulness enables us to notice when past attachment wounds are triggered, helping us to pause before reacting impulsively. By cultivating this awareness, we create space for intentional responses that align with our healing goals and nourish our relationships.

Healing through compassion

As we explore our attachment wounds through self-reflection, we may encounter feelings of sadness, regret, or frustration. Embracing self-compassion means meeting these feelings with warmth and understanding, just as we would offer comfort to a dear friend. Rather than criticizing ourselves for past behaviors or perceived shortcomings, self-compassion encourages us to embrace our humanity and respond with love and care. By extending this compassion inward, we heal the wounds of self-judgment and create a foundation for self-acceptance and emotional healing.

The Journey of Discovery

The process of self-reflection is not linear, but cyclical, much like the ebb and flow of the tides. There will be moments of clarity and breakthrough, as well as times of challenge and uncertainty. Embracing self-reflection as an ongoing journey invites us to view each experience as an opportunity for growth. With a gentle and patient approach, we can navigate the complexities of healing, trusting that each step we take brings us closer to emotional liberation and authentic connection.

Empowerment and transformation

Ultimately, self-reflection empowers us to become agents of change in our lives. Through self-reflection, we reclaim the power to rewrite the narratives that have shaped our attachment style and relationships. Armed with self-awareness and understanding, we can challenge old scripts and choose responses that align with our desired emotional landscape. Empowerment comes from the realization that we are not defined by our past, and transformation is possible when we embrace our capacity for growth and resilience.

Practical cues for self-reflection

Before engaging in self-reflection, find a quiet place, clear your mind, and grab a pen and paper. Create an environment conducive to introspection and allow yourself to explore your thoughts and feelings with focus and clarity. To engage in self-reflection, ask yourself the following questions:

1. What emotions and thoughts arise when I think about past experiences with caregivers or past relationships?

2. How do I typically respond in intimate relationships when faced with feelings of vulnerability or insecurity?

3. Are there patterns or recurring triggers in my relationships that seem related to my early attachment experiences?

4. What attachment behaviors do I find myself engaging in, such as seeking reassurance or withdrawing emotionally? How do these behaviors impact my relationships?

5. How do I view myself and my worthiness for love and care in light of my attachment style?

6. Are there specific memories or events from my childhood that I believe have influenced my attachment style?

7. How has my attachment style affected my overall emotional well-being and the quality of my relationships?

8. How can I practice self-compassion and self-acceptance as I explore and address my attachment wounds?

9. What steps can I take to create a safe and supportive environment for my healing journey?

10. How can I apply mindfulness to my daily interactions to become more

aware of my emotional responses and attachment-related patterns?

Remember that self-reflection is a process of gentle exploration and there are no right or wrong answers. Use these questions as a starting point to gain deeper insights into your attachment style and to take meaningful steps toward healing and growth. Consider keeping a journal to document your reflections and track your progress on this transformative journey.

Emotional Regulation: Nurturing Inner Harmony to Heal Attachment Wounds

Learning to regulate emotions is essential for people with attachment wounds. Emotionally charged responses rooted in past experiences can interfere with effective communication and connection with others. Techniques such as mindfulness, deep breathing, and grounding exercises can help individuals manage overwhelming emotions and respond more calmly and authentically in relationships.

The impact of unregulated emotions

Unresolved attachment wounds can lead to heightened emotional reactivity in relationships. Past experiences of neglect, abandonment, or inconsistency can lead to intense feelings of fear, anxiety, or anger when faced with situations that trigger these unresolved emotions. Such emotional intensity can disrupt communication and contribute to conflict or separation in relationships.

The role of emotional regulation

Emotional regulation is the ability to recognize, understand, and effectively manage our emotional responses. For individuals with attachment wounds, emotional regulation plays a critical role in breaking free from automatic, fear-based responses that stem from past experiences. By developing emotional awareness and regulation skills, individuals can respond to present situations more consciously and with less emotional interference from unresolved wounds. Here are some valuable emotion regulation strategies that can bring comfort and release during challenging emotional experiences:

Engage in physical activities

Physical activity provides an excellent outlet for processing and releasing pent-up emotions. Engaging in exercises such as taking a brisk walk, jogging, dancing, or practicing yoga can help release tension and promote a sense of calm. Physical movement stimulates the release of endorphins, which are natural mood enhancers, and promotes a more balanced emotional state. Whether it's done alone or with others, physical movement can be an effective way to ground yourself and connect with your body.

Example:

- Go for a 30-minute brisk walk or jog in a nearby park or nature trail.

- Join a dance class or dance to your favorite music at home.

- Practice yoga or participate in online yoga sessions for relaxation and grounding.

- Play a sport you enjoy, such as basketball, tennis, or soccer, to release tension and boost your mood.

Creative expression

Creative activities provide a safe space for emotional expression and exploration. Engaging in artistic activities such as drawing, painting, writing, or playing a musical instrument can help you channel emotions into tangible forms of self-expression. Creativity allows you to process complex emotions that may be difficult to articulate verbally. The act of creating art can be cathartic, fostering a sense of release and empowerment.

Example:

- Set aside time to draw or paint your emotions on paper or canvas.

- Start a journal and write about your feelings, thoughts, and experiences.

- Play a musical instrument or create music to express emotions without words.

- Engage in a creative writing exercise, such as free-writing or poetry, to process and articulate your emotions.

Mindful meditation

Mindful meditation is a powerful emotion regulation practice. By taking time to focus on the present moment and observe your thoughts and feelings without judgment, you cultivate emotional awareness and develop the ability to respond more intentionally to emotional triggers. Regular mindfulness meditation helps you build resilience and enhances your ability to navigate emotions with grace and compassion.

Example:

- Find a quiet space, sit comfortably, and focus on your breath. Practice mindful breathing for 5-10 minutes each day.

- Try guided mindfulness meditation apps or videos to support your meditation practice.

- Incorporate mindfulness into everyday activities, such as mindful eating or mindful walking, to bring awareness to the present moment.

Breathwork techniques

Conscious breathing exercises, such as deep breathing or diaphragmatic breathing, can quickly calm the nervous system and reduce stress. Focusing on the breath helps to shift your attention away from distressing emotions, promoting relaxation and emotional balance. Incorporating breathwork into your daily routine can serve as a reliable tool for managing emotional intensity.

Example:

- Practice deep breathing exercises: Inhale deeply through your nose for a count of 4, hold for 4 counts, and exhale slowly for 4 counts. Repeat several times.

- Try diaphragmatic breathing: Place one hand on your chest and the other on your abdomen. Inhale deeply, allowing your abdomen to expand, and exhale slowly, feeling your abdomen contract.

Create a calming space

Designating a specific area in your home as a calming space can provide a retreat for self-reflection and emotional regulation. Fill this space with calming elements, such as soft lighting, soothing scents, or objects that evoke positive emotions.

This space can serve as a sanctuary where you can process emotions, engage in mindfulness practices, or simply find comfort during turbulent times.

Example:

- Choose a corner in your room or a small area in your home to create your calming space.

- Decorate it with items that bring you comfort, such as soft cushions, candles, or calming artwork.

- Use this space for meditation, relaxation, or to engage in creative activities that help regulate your emotions.

Supportive social connections

Building a supportive social network can be an important aspect of emotion regulation. Cultivate relationships with people who understand and validate your emotions and provide a safe space to share your feelings. Whether it's through conversation, shared activities, or simply being present for one another, supportive social connections contribute to emotional well-being.

Example:

- Reach out to friends or family members who understand and support you emotionally.

- Engage in meaningful conversations with loved ones, sharing your feelings and actively listening to theirs.

- Participate in group activities or virtual gatherings to foster a sense of community and connection.

Take breaks and time-outs

Recognize the importance of self-care and take breaks or time-outs when needed. Stepping away from challenging situations allows you to collect your thoughts and emotions, preventing impulsive reactions and encouraging more thoughtful responses.

Example:

- When you feel overwhelmed, step outside or find a quiet room to take a few moments to yourself.

- Practice deep breathing during your time-out to center yourself and regain emotional balance.

- Use this time to reflect on your emotions and identify any triggers or patterns that may be arising.

Please remember that the key to effective emotion regulation is to experiment with these strategies and discover what works best for you. Be curious and patient as you explore these activities, and don't hesitate to adapt or combine them to meet your unique needs and preferences. Consistency is key, so aim to incorporate these practices into your daily routine to empower yourself to navigate emotions with greater resilience and cultivate emotional well-being in your relationships and daily life.

Connect with Your Inner Child: Embracing Compassion and Healing from Within

Connecting with your inner child may sound like a deep and introspective process, but it can be a profoundly rewarding journey that brings healing and understanding to your emotional world. Are you ready for this adventure of self-discovery? Let's dive in!

The healing power of reconnecting with your inner child

Think back to your childhood. Can you picture your younger self, full of innocence and curiosity? Take a moment to visualize this precious version of yourself. This visualization allows you to reconnect with your early experiences and see how they may have influenced your emotional responses and attachment style today.

Understand emotional needs and vulnerabilities

As you explore the world of your inner child, try to understand its emotional needs and vulnerabilities. What experiences may have shaped the way you view love, trust, and security? Be patient and gentle with yourself as you delve into these memories. It's a journey of self-compassion, and you have the power to embrace all aspects of your past.

Be compassionate and nurturing

Imagine being the caring and nurturing adult figure for your younger self. Extend the same love and support that you would give to a child facing emotional challenges. Your inner child deserves this compassion, and you have the capacity to offer it.

Acknowledge feelings and experiences

Sometimes memories from the past can bring up strong emotions. That's perfectly okay. Allow yourself to feel and process these feelings. It's part of the healing process. Remember that you are here to hold space for your inner child and to offer comfort and understanding.

The Gift of self-compassion

Being kind to yourself is a transformative gift you can offer. Embracing your inner child with self-compassion means accepting yourself fully, including your vulnerabilities and imperfections. It's about recognizing that you are worthy of the love and understanding you would willingly give to others.

Incorporating inner child work into daily life

Inner child work doesn't have to be limited to deep introspection sessions. You can bring this practice into your everyday life. When you encounter moments of emotional intensity or relationship triggers, pause and connect with your inner child. Ask yourself what emotional needs are arising and how you can respond to them with love and care.

Action Step: Embrace Your Inner Child Meditation

1. Find a quiet place: Set aside some time and find a quiet place where you won't be disturbed.

2. Get comfortable: Sit in a comfortable position, either in a chair or on the floor, with your back straight. You can also lie down if it feels more relaxing.

3. Close your eyes: Gently close your eyes to shut out outside distractions and focus inward.

4. Take deep breaths: Begin by taking a few deep breaths. Inhale slowly through your nose, hold for a moment, and exhale through your mouth.

Feel yourself becoming more relaxed with each breath.

5. Visualize your younger self: As you continue to take deep breaths, imagine yourself at a certain age in your childhood. Picture your younger self with clarity, remembering your facial expressions and body language.

6. Extend love and compassion: Offer your younger self love and compassion. Imagine yourself as the nurturing and caring adult figure you needed at that age. Speak kind and reassuring words to your inner child, letting him know that you are here for him and that he is safe.

7. Acknowledge emotions: Allow any emotions that arise to be present without judgment. If you feel sadness, fear, or any other emotion, let it flow. Embrace these emotions with the same understanding and tenderness you would offer a child.

8. Listen and comfort: Take a moment to listen to the needs and feelings of your inner child. Comfort them and let them know that their feelings are valid and accepted.

9. Embrace the connection: Feel the connection between your present self and your inner child grow stronger with each breath. Embrace the feeling of love and understanding that flows through this connection.

10. Gratitude and closure: Before ending the meditation, express gratitude to your inner child for sharing this experience with you. Imagine giving your younger self a warm hug and feeling a sense of comfort and healing.

11. Slowly return: When you are ready, slowly bring your awareness back to the present moment. Gently open your eyes and take a moment to ground yourself.

The Journey of Wholeness

Remember, this journey of connecting with your inner child is an ongoing one. It's about nurturing a sense of wholeness within yourself. As you nurture your inner child, you strengthen your emotional resilience and lay the foundation for healthier relationships and emotional well-being.

Therapy and Counseling

Seeking professional therapy is an important step in the healing process. A skilled therapist can provide a safe and supportive environment to explore past attachment experiences, identify emotional triggers, and work through unresolved feelings. Therapists can use a variety of evidence-based techniques and approaches to help individuals process their emotions, reframe negative beliefs, and develop healthier attachment patterns.

There are several approaches that therapists can use to help individuals effectively work through their attachment issues. Here are some of the most commonly used and evidence-based therapeutic approaches:

- **Emotionally Focused Therapy (EFT):** EFT is a widely accepted and empirically validated approach specifically designed to address attachment issues in couples therapy. It focuses on helping individuals identify and express their underlying emotions and needs in a safe and supportive environment. The therapist assists clients in understanding their attachment styles and how these patterns affect their interactions with their partners. Through the process of emotional exploration and expression, couples can create a more secure and fulfilling relationship.

- **Attachment Based Therapy:** As the name suggests, attachment-based therapy directly targets attachment-related challenges. This therapeutic approach recognizes the importance of early attachment experiences and how they shape a person's attachment style. The therapist works with individuals to identify and understand the impact of these experiences on their current relationships and emotional well-being. Attachment therapy often involves exploring attachment wounds, providing corrective emotional experiences, and fostering more secure attachment patterns.

- **Cognitive Behavioral Therapy (CBT):** CBT is a versatile therapeutic approach that can be adapted to address attachment wounds. It focuses on identifying and challenging negative thought patterns and beliefs stemming from early attachment experiences. The therapist helps the individual reframe negative beliefs and develop healthier coping strategies and relationship behaviors. By targeting cognitive and behavioral aspects, CBT can be effective in promoting positive changes in attachment styles and relationship dynamics.

- **Psychodynamic Therapy:** Psychodynamic therapy addresses a person's unconscious thoughts and feelings, including those related to attachment experiences. By exploring early childhood memories and experiences, individuals can gain insight into the root causes of their attachment wounds and emotional struggles. Psychodynamic therapy helps clients process unresolved feelings and develop a deeper understanding of how past experiences influence their current relationships and sense of self.

- **Eye Movement Desensitization and Reprocessing (EMDR):** EMDR is a specialized therapeutic approach used primarily to address trauma-related issues. For individuals with attachment wounds resulting from traumatic experiences, EMDR can be beneficial in processing and integrating these traumas. By targeting distressing memories and emotions, EMDR helps individuals reduce the emotional charge associated with past traumatic events, thereby promoting emotional healing and resilience.

- **Mindfulness-Based Therapies:** Mindfulness-based therapies, such as Mindfulness-Based Stress Reduction (MBSR) and Mindfulness-Based Cognitive Therapy (MBCT), can complement other therapeutic approaches in healing attachment wounds. Mindfulness practices promote self-awareness, emotional regulation, and self-compassion. By cultivating mindfulness, individuals can learn to respond more skillfully to emotional triggers and reduce reactive behaviors that result from attachment wounds.

Ultimately, the choice of therapeutic approach depends on the individual's unique needs, preferences, and specific attachment-related challenges. A skilled therapist will tailor the treatment plan to the individual's specific attachment style and experiences, ensuring that the therapy is aligned with the individual's goals and helps them achieve positive outcomes.

Healing attachment wounds requires self-reflection, emotional regulation, inner-child work, and professional therapy.

- Self-reflection: This means understanding the impact of past experiences on our attachment style and behaviors.

- Emotional regulation: This means learning how to manage overwhelming emotions and respond authentically in our relationships.

- Inner child work: This means connecting with our inner child and developing compassion and understanding for ourselves.

- Professional therapy: This can be helpful when we need support to heal from past trauma or to learn new skills.

Healing attachment wounds is a journey, not a destination. It takes time and effort, but it is possible to create healthier relationships and emotional well-being.

Conclusion

Congratulations on reaching the conclusion of this captivating journey! If you've made it this far, it's evident that you are truly invested in transforming your romantic relationships and enriching your inner self. As we wrap up this enlightening exploration of insecure attachment, let us take a moment to reflect on the profound insights and valuable lessons we've gathered along the way.

Throughout this book, we have explored the effects of insecure attachment on relationships, such as communication breakdowns, trust issues, and the tendency to seek constant reassurance. Insecure attachment can be a complex emotional state, often stemming from past experiences, and it can lead to challenges in connecting with our partners.

However, by exploring these issues, we've gained valuable insights and tools to address them effectively. We've learned the importance of open communication, honest self-reflection, and striking a balance between sharing our feelings and respecting our partner's boundaries. Through self-improvement, we can shed harmful patterns and embrace positive changes, fostering an environment of trust and understanding.

By acknowledging and understanding our insecurities, we take the first step toward healing and growth. It's important to realize that a relationship riddled with fear and insecurity is not the most promising. However, with commitment and self-compassion, we can overcome our fears and embrace the present, enjoying our relationships for what they are, in the here and now.

But this is not the end; it's just the beginning of your journey to healthier relationships and personal growth. I encourage you to celebrate yourself for taking these steps to better understand yourself and your connections with others. Celebrate your willingness to explore your vulnerabilities and work toward becoming the best version of yourself.

As you move forward, I invite you to revisit the parts of this book that resonate most with you. Take time to reflect, absorb, and apply the insights you've gained. Each step you take brings you closer to creating the fulfilling and loving relationships you deserve.

Keep in mind that growth takes time, and setbacks are a natural part of the process. Be patient with yourself and celebrate each milestone, no matter how small. Embrace the lessons of both your successes and your challenges, for they all contribute to your growth.

There is no shame in admitting that you need help. If you find that past problems are affecting your present, or you're struggling to overcome your fears, seeking professional help and support is a powerful and courageous step. Talking to your partner can be a great place to start, helping them understand what's going on in your head and opening the door to support. If needed, there are other options such as couples therapy, individual therapy, and self-help methods that can help you overcome anxiety.

Don't let anxiety hold you back or derail your life. Face your fears, overcome them, and look forward to a future free of constant relationship insecurity and anxiety. You deserve love, happiness and fulfilling relationships, and with your commitment and determination, you will achieve just that.

Thank you for joining me on this transformative journey. Keep celebrating yourself, keep learning, and keep growing. Here's to your brighter, happier, more love-filled future! Good luck on your journey ahead!

www.ingramcontent.com/pod-product-compliance
Lightning Source LLC
LaVergne TN
LVHW021817060526
838201LV00058B/3424